I Love You The Same

Phillip & Rosemary Mata

I Love You The Same ©2021 by Phillip & Rosemary Mata
All rights reserved. No part of this book may be reproduced in any form without permission in writing from Phillip & Rosemary Mata

Printed in the United States of America

First Printing: December 2021

ISBN-13: 978-1-7324084-5-6

100-Fold-Life Publishing

Dedication

To our children April Lynn Mata Cloudt and Jonathan Mata, our grandchildren: Noah Alan Cloudt, Ezekiel Phillip Cloudt, and Ruby Mata.

We also acknowledge our beloved extended family, The Matas and The Garcias.

With a special mention of honor to our church family, at the Church of Living Waters. Pastor Darren and Gamila Frank. Thank you all for loving us, growing us all these years.

Table of Contents

Dedication ii
Table of Contents iii
Introduction iv
1 My Early Years 1
2 Mi Familia 5
3 My Education 17
4 Enter Rosemary 21
5 The Great Elope 25
6 Growing Pains 39
7 My Road to Damascus 43
8 New Wine Skin 49
9 The White Dress 57
Photo Album 65
10 Miracles Can And Will Happen 69
11 Becoming Patents 81
12 The Upper Room 89
13 God Is In The Details 95
14 Rosemary's Funeral 109
15 The Resurrection Power 119
Epilogue 125

Introduction

'I love you the same' started out by being an expression that I would sign my name to in letters and cards that I wrote to Rosemary. It simply meant regardless of our hurts, unkind words and deeds towards each other, whether we were struggling or in times of great rejoicing, *"I love you the same."* As the song says, *"I Never Lost That Loving Feeling."* But as we grew in God, we discovered His love was the same for us. It never failed. It never gave up. He too loved us the same.

I always wanted to write a book to honor God and what He has done in my life. My heart's desire in writing, *I Love You The Same*, my story, is to share my ups and downs, my insecurities, my mistakes, and my past to give you hope. To show off my God and how good and faithful He is. You can have a new identity, a new purpose, and a new future free from your past all through the Lord and Savior Jesus Christ.

> "However, as it is written: "What no eye has seen, what no ear has heard, and what no human mind has conceived" the things God has prepared for those who love him these are the things God has revealed to us by his Spirit. The Spirit searches all things, even the deep things of God. For who knows a person's thoughts except their own spirit within them? In the same way no one knows the thoughts of God except the Spirit of God. What we have received is not the spirit of the world, but the Spirit who is from God, so that we may understand what God has freely given us. This is what we speak, not in words taught us by human wisdom

> *but in words taught by the Spirit, explaining spiritual realities with Spirit-taught words. The person without the Spirit does not accept the things that come from the Spirit of God but considers them foolishness and cannot understand them because they are discerned only through the Spirit. The person with the Spirit makes judgments about all things, but such a person is not subject to merely human judgments." 1 Corinthians 2:9-15*

So, no matter what you did or didn't do yesterday or today, right now God is saying to you,

I love you the same.

Don't allow the enemy to keep you from a relationship with God for another second of your life. God is not sitting on His throne in heaven wagging his finger at you or criticizing you for the things that you have done. He's sitting there looking at you with love-filled eyes and his arms stretched out to you saying, "Come to me. There is nothing that can keep me from loving you, my child."

> *"For I am convinced that neither death nor life, neither angels nor demons, neither the present nor the future, nor any powers, neither height nor depth, nor anything else in all creation, will be able to separate us from the love of God that is in Christ Jesus our Lord." Rm 8:38-39*

"For God so loved the world that He gave His only begotten Son, that whoever believes in Him should not perish but have everlasting life. For God did not send His Son into the world to condemn the world, but that the world through Him might be saved." John 3:16-17

1

My Early Years

I was born in a town called Richmond, Texas on October 20th, 1960, to my parents, Gilbert and Emily Mata, who lived in Rosenberg, Texas, a few miles away. We lived on what was considered the north side of town, "across the tracks." We lived in a little small house across the street from a little white Catholic church where we attended mass every Sunday. It was a friendly, quaint town where everyone knew each other or were related to each other. You had to be careful who you dated because they just may end up being your relative. It was a tight-knit community filled with love.

I don't have a ton of childhood memories, but a few things that I remember most about my childhood are that I was really small and my parents playing Spanish music all throughout the house. My mom would put me on her feet and hold my hands so I could feel like we were dancing. I remember just loving her so much and looking up to her and telling her, "Someday I'm gonna marry you, Mom." She'd just smile and say "No, Phillip, I am already married to your dad. You will have your own wife someday." That is honestly the only mention of my future I recall my parents speaking to me about as a youth. The other memory that brings a smile to my face was when I pretended to be Batman. I would run around in a towel for a cape and a pair of Batman boots. Lol, I loved those Batman boots. I also remember swimming in the river with a dangerous current, the Brazos River. Brazos means "the arms of God." Even back then, God was stretching his arm out and protecting me. He loved me the same.

In 1971, my dad leased a bar call Gilbert's Bar and Pool, but we called it "The Place." It was actually more of a beer joint than a bar. While my dad was running Gilbert's, my Mom worked the night shift at a senior citizens home. I remember seeing her studying at the kitchen table all the time. She slept during the day and stayed out all night. A few months later, I remember feeling like something changed in the house. Suddenly, there was no more laughter and no more singing and dancing to the Spanish music. Prior to my dad buying the bar, he worked at a grocery store. He seemed happy there but maybe he wasn't. I don't know, but when this opportunity arose, he jumped on it.

Once they opened the bar, I immediately became responsible for myself. I was around eleven years old. I had to do my homework, feed myself, and put myself to sleep. I remember this one night I was so hungry that I tried to cook bacon on the stove by myself. The next thing I know, I was taking it out the pan and trying to eat it. It was still raw, but I didn't care, my stomach hurt, and I wanted to fill it. I began to cry as it burned my tongue but kept on eating it. I was just too hungry to wait for it to finish cooking.

I have a younger sister, too, but for the most part she was raised by the babysitter. She was with the babysitter more than our parents, so I only visited with her sometimes on the weekend. I remember being young and calling my grandparents and telling them a little white lie because I didn't want to be home alone anymore. I wanted someone to come tell my parents to take care of me and to feed me. I just wanted to go back to being a family and I wanted to be taken care of. That didn't work out the way I planned at all. After I called them, grandma and grandpa came over. I remember sitting on my floor playing with my toys and my mom crying and my dad with his head down just saying "okay-okay" to my grandparents who told them they were going to take me home to be with them to Houston, Texas, an hour away.

"What?!" I could not believe that. In my mind, they were just getting rid of me as if I was the problem. These were my father's parents. My grandpa was from Mexico and my grandma was from Shiner, Texas. They were kind people that lived in a wooden home that they built. They owned several homes and apartments. Grandpa did real estate and did really well. He served others and helped people who didn't have a place to live or food to eat. They were very beautiful, loving and giving people. My grandmother raised eight children. Their home was always warm and inviting. I always remember her in the kitchen cooking something great. You always smelled rice, beans, and tortillas cooking. Every breakfast, lunch, and dinner grandma made homemade fresh tortillas that she would cook with cheese and put on top of your dish as your treat.

As a young boy I even remember going with my cousins and picking up bottles and cans so that we could go and get some money for ourselves. I started to grow up too fast. I wanted to have money and things for myself. I was smoking on the weekends by twelve years old. I remember this one time my grandma getting on my grandpa saying, "Hey, that's enough already. "You're drinking too much beer today." His response was a giggle and he said "Hey, I'm not really drinking the beer because I want to, I'm trying to help these boys here make some extra money. They were proud people, good people, but I never heard, "I love you" from them. It was always implied in everything that they did and in the way that they took care of you. Their generosity was overwhelming.

2

Mi Familia

> *"Honor your father and your mother, so that you may live long in the land the LORD your God is giving you.*
> *Exodus 20:12*

Mi Padre

My dad was born September 1st, 1937, in Wharton, Texas. Two years later, on September 3rd, 1939, he moved to East Texas. Dad only went to school till the ninth grade and started picking cotton in Odessa, Texas at 15. Odessa gets very hot so you have to pick cotton picking early in the morning to do it. "It will keep you from getting cut," is what my father told me. I never knew he had it so hard and that he had to do that when he was younger. My parents married when my dad was 21 and my mom was 19. When he was born, he was a preemie baby. When I was born, I was a preemie baby. And when my son, Jonathan, was born, he was a preemie baby. My father told me he was so small when he was born, his mother had to put him in a shoe box with a whole bunch of cotton all around him to keep him warm. My father was a boy with dreams. He was an altar boy in the church. He loved baseball. He picked cotton and he went to school till the 9th grade. He was a hardworking man. When I was young, before the bar, he worked at a grocery store. From 1953 to 1970, he worked at Love's Food Market. I know he was a very hard-working man, but something happened to him at work where he wasn't treated fairly, and from that moment, he dreamed of being his own boss. So, when he was given the opportunity to buy property from my aunt in 1970, he went for it. This is about the time when I went to live with my grandparents in 1972. That's when he became the "boss." So, when it came time for him to own his own place, he worked even harder. He was never home. That place became "his place," the only place he ever was. That place also came with a price. First, he lost his children-my sister was raised by the babysitter and I had to go live with my grandparents-and later, he had a child out of wedlock that led to him divorcing my mom.

My father had a softball team he loved hanging out with. I think that's why he called the bar, The Place, because to him. It was more than a bar, it was a place for people to gather, eat food and drink, and to spend time together. Gilbert's A's softball team was primarily made up of customers and friends that loved baseball. Jokingly, we called ourselves the Alcoholic A's because win or lose, we knew how to celebrate. I played catcher on the team when I was 17 and 18 years old. Baseball is one of the few hobbies that my dad and I had in common.

    I'm not telling you any of this to put my father down, I'm telling you this because I'm learning now my father was just a man. He was hurting, he was lost, and he was doing the best that he could. In his mind, and in a lot of men's minds, the best way to be a good man is to provide, to go to work morning, noon, and night. Even me. After I got saved, after God did all that restoring to me, I still worked every bit of overtime I could. I still thought it was important that I provide a good home for my family; that I made sure that we had enough money; that we were able to buy land and build a home later. But what our children need the most *is us*. They need us men to show them they're loved, to teach them they're loved, to teach them how to love, to teach them how to be men and women, to discipline them in a loving way, and most importantly, to show them the love of God and to teach them about their Savior Jesus Christ. None of us are perfect and none of us can do this world without Christ.

> *"... for all have sinned and fall short of the glory of God."* Romans 3:23

We are always going to fall short when we do it in and of ourselves. Because Jesus first loved us. He has always loved us the same. One thing we have in common is we are all fighters; we protect what is ours. We all have good in us. We all have the ability to grow and change. We are all made in the image of God, and we are all God's children.

Even though me and my sister didn't grow up together in the same home, we have decided to be closer now. My sister asked me to take my dad to the doctor the other day because she lives with him and cares for him daily, so I took my dad to the doctor. We have been spending a lot of time together lately. I love baseball, the Houston Astros specifically. As we watched a few Astros games together, I started to see my father as a real person. I now see him as a man that really tried his best to provide for his family and to do the best he could, but he paid a price. He paid a price for a lot of his mistakes, but mostly for not surrendering his life to the Lord. He lived for himself. God's always aware of our hearts desire so even though we were not close when I was young, I'm now 60 and he's 83, we are all finally having conversations.

Mi Madre

Right now, as we speak, my mother is in a convalescent home. She has lived a long life. She suffered from her own battle with alcohol and a failing marriage but eventually she came to know the Lord.

My mom used to stand at the window washing her dishes waiting for the school bus to drop off the kids wishing and praying I would be getting off of that bus. I never did because I had gone to live with my grandparents, something she never wanted. She wept openly about this even on the night that my grandparents were there. I remember they were sitting on my bed. I was on the floor and my dad kept saying "okay" and my mom was just weeping. I didn't understand her weeping. I thought she was letting me go. I thought she didn't want me. I thought I'd burdened her, but her tears were not for that at all. Her tears were because she felt like she failed me as a mom and all she wanted was for me to come home. I didn't learn this till much later in life when she shared with me her story. I had been so angry and hurt, I resented her for many years.

We think we know the beginning from the end. We think we understand all the things our parents have done. But in all honesty, we really don't. We don't know the man's/woman's heart.

"For what man knows the things of a man except the spirit of the man which is in him? Even so no one knows the things of God except the Spirit of God." 1 Corinthians 2:11

My dad's bar took my mom's dreams from her. She didn't want to be a bar owner; she wanted to be a nurse. I remember her being up late at night studying all the time, but she never got to fulfill her dream of being a nurse.

I hate to say it, but when I first got saved, I still hated my mom. Even though she wept when I left, I felt like she didn't ever say "no." She never said, "Don't take him." I blamed her. I don't know why as children we do those things. I never blamed my father, but I did blame her. I think it's because my grandparents made my father seem so wonderful and no one was sticking up for my mom. As an adult I have repented to her. I have so much love for my mother. I have forgiven her for that day and for any other thing that she may have done or didn't do. I now know she did the best job she could under the circumstances. I know that I was ugly to her, and I have truly repented and asked for her forgiveness. And she has graciously given it to me.

One of my most memorable days was October 1988, two years into my walk with the Lord. God spoke to me about my heart and my mom. I had a dream of sorts. I heard God audibly say, "Phillip, today you're going to find your mom on the kitchen floor dead." My heart skipped a beat. My heart instantly softened, and I cried out to God, "No, please God, give me a chance to go back and make things right with her. To forgive her, and to ask her to forgive me." Then I left for work, but all day long every time I heard the phone ring, I prayed, "God, don't let her die." She was on my mind all day long. So much so that as soon as work was over, I went to her house and found her in the kitchen drunk as a skunk. I begged her to forgive me, and she just said, "Yeah, yeah, yeah." So, I told her the story about pastor's brother-in-law who went to Vietnam and then got delivered from heroin. He's having meetings on Wednesdays. I asked her if she would come with me and hear this man speak for ten consecutive Wednesdays. She said, "No, I'm born Catholic, I'm going to die Catholic." "I'm not here to take you out of your church," I said, "I just want you to come hear this man speak." She said, "Okay." I said, "No, for real." She said, "Okay."

Tuesday came and Rosemary called me at work and said, "Your mom called." My heart skipped a beat again. I hope she's okay. All I could think was my mom was canceling for tomorrow. Rosemary said, "Your mom said, "Don't forget to pick her up on Wednesday." I sighed a sigh of relief knowing that God was at work and that all of this was in God's timing, not my own. Wednesday night came around and I picked her up. After two Wednesdays, she said, "Don't bring me here anymore." I said, "Huh? Why?" There must be a mistake. She said, "The speaker said I need to go someplace else like AA or something like that." I said, "No, Mom, I think you misunderstood. I want you to keep coming on Wednesday." The speaker clarified what he told her and she kept her word. But as the ten weeks came to an end, she was the only one left in the meeting in that prayer house. And on that day, the last Wednesday, she got delivered. After that, she came to church on Sundays for about ten and a half years and then she moved on with her group of women that she is now with today. She later said, "When I die, please take me to the Catholic Church and to Living Waters. But in these last few weeks she's told me, "No, just take me to Living Waters." God is so good. His love is always the same. It never changes.

My mom has told me a lot of stories about things that I never knew about, like inviting my friends to come watch her Tv just so she could feel close to me. She also told me the story about waiting in that window praying I would get off that school bus. As children we can be so critical and self-absorbed that we overlook the fact that our parents are human beings, too. They feel and hurt and struggle, too.

My aunt was so thrilled when she found out that her sister had given her life to the Lord. My aunt led us to the Lord; I led my mom to the Lord. God always gets his man and his woman, so don't ever think your prayers are in vain. God is going to do things His way and in his timing. Trust God, trust the process, "do not lean on your own understanding," and watch and see what the Lord does in your life. I always refer to this scripture:

> *"Trust in the Lord with all your heart,*
> *And lean not on your own understanding;*
> *In all your ways acknowledge Him,*
> *And He shall direct your paths." Proverbs 3:5-6*

For he truly does love us the same.

Once my mom was set free, she was so full of joy. She would dance for the Lord unashamed just like David did in the Bible. She would be the first one in that first row to jump to her feet and dance. She would grab anybody and everybody that was next to her to dance with her.

> *"So David said to Michal, "It was before the Lord, who chose me instead of your father and all his house, to appoint me ruler over the people of the Lord, over Israel. Therefore I will play music before the Lord. And I will be even more undignified than this, and will be humble in my own sight. But as for the maidservants of whom you have spoken, by them I will be held in honor." 2 Samuel 6:21-22*

God set her free from cigarettes as well. One Sunday, the pastor's wife was speaking to this woman sitting in front of my mom, "You are set free from those cigarettes right now!" My mom thought she was talking to her, so she raised her hands, received the pastor's word, and she too was set free from cigarettes the same day.

God has always been in the details in my stories. Everything comes full circle and God always gets the glory. What I learned that day and every day since then in my latter years is there are always two sides to every story. I can't just choose a side. I have to hear both sides and I have to choose to stay in the middle, which is the side of God. God is so good. First, he introduced me to that prayer house where I got baptized in the fire, and two years later, my mom gave her life to the Lord there and she got set free in the same way. But God.

Mi Hermana

Corina is my younger sister. We were not close growing up, but we are very close now. She has four children, my nieces, Miranda and Jessica, and two nephews, Joshua and Noah. She works at a department store. She still attends Catholic Church and loves God. Like I stated, we missed a lot of each other growing up, but we talk now a lot about forgiveness. I share the love of Christ with her often and just how good God has been to me and to my family. I share my testimonies with her and what inspires me to go to church as often as I do. I just can't stop telling her what

God has done to me and for me. I can never thank Him enough for his faithfulness.

I know she's close to my dad. She worked a lot in the bar growing up and saw a lot of things, so her walk is very different than mine, yet, we are family and I love her very much. I chose to keep myself away from the bar because I didn't want to be "in the way." My dad had his daughter and his two small boys from another woman, so I never really felt like I fit in. I never really felt like I belonged even after being saved. I didn't feel loved by them. So, of course, when I gave my life to the Lord, the last thing I wanted to do was be in a bar. I didn't want anything more to do with alcohol. For me, I just felt like I had to separate myself from that environment and get closer to God so that I could tend to my marriage and put my focus into my family, my wife, and later, my two precious children.

I knew the only way to be around my mom and my dad was to be at the bar, but for me, that was just not an option. I wanted a different life that was all about God who loved me despite my flaws. I wanted it so bad that I even told my sister that when it comes down to our parents passing and it's time to inherit the bar, I will turn it into a church and call it "The Place of New Beginnings in Jesus Christ," laughing of course because it's not just my decision, but mine and my sister's decision. I know my Aunt Lorene gave that bar to my mom and dad in hopes that they would know that there was a good God, in hopes that it would bring them closer together. And I know it would bring her peace to know that that place was now a church, especially after that place had brought so much division to my parents.

"And we know that all things work together for good to those who love God, to those who are the called according to His purpose." Romans 8:28

3

My Education

*"Train up a child in the way he should go,
And when he is old he will not depart from it."* Proverbs 22:6

Most of my school years were difficult. I started out with Ds and Fs because I was always trying to study by myself. Most of the time I was hungry, tired, or I just wasn't even disciplined enough to know how to manage my time well and to study for myself. I remember even trying to ask my parents to help me with spelling and putting words into sentences. I remember all my mom said to me was "go and get the dictionary and learn for yourself." I thought, wow, how can I look up the word correctly and find it in the dictionary if I don't know how to spell it? I was trying so hard to get an A on one of my spelling tests so that I could get a piece of bubble gum. I didn't get an A, but I did get a B. So, my teacher gave me two pieces of bubble gum because she saw my efforts. In our house, my parents didn't speak Spanish to us much, mostly English, so that we would do better and have a better life than what they had. They worked hard and left me all alone. They would buy me things, but all the while, all I wanted was their time, their presence, their love, and their affection. I do long to hear the words, *I love you.* Now I know my love language is words of affirmation, but for this little boy, he just wanted to be loved. Yes, my parents were hardworking, and at that time when I was young, I just felt so alone. But now looking back, I realize that they just wanted to be their own boss and to have something that they could be proud of, even if it was just a bar.

Junior high was interesting for me as well. I remember being bullied by a big guy and thinking to myself, "I got to learn how to fight and take care of myself." So, I asked one of my friends to go to the Black Belt Academy to learn karate and self-defense. I didn't make it past the white belt but I did learn enough to defend myself. I ended up beating that bully up and that took care of that. From that point on, everybody was told, "You better leave that boy, Phillip, alone because he doesn't play around." I didn't get into trouble, but I also didn't have friends or play sports. I just kind of tried to get through school as best as I could. I know that a lot of the kids that I went to school with seemed bigger than me. I just wanted to hurry up and finish school so I could get a job and start working. In hindsight, I was frustrated with my parents for always working, yet, I could not wait to get a job myself.

By high school, I was wearing my hair long. It was all the way down to my shoulders. I wore Converse Chucks, jeans, and an army shirt. I was not popular nor was I trying to be, but I did want to fit in. I just wanted to get my education so I could work. That's all I knew. I was looking forward to going back to my original school so I could graduate with all my friends. It was a promise I made to myself. Something to look forward to after being separated from my parents.

My first job was at Taco Bell. I rode a ten-speed bicycle for ten miles. I lied on my application that I was already sixteen. I just wanted a job so bad I even went and cut my hair off after the interview in hopes that I would get that job. When they called me and told me I got it, I couldn't believe it. I went to that job the next day with a fresh new haircut and my boss didn't even recognize me. I was so proud of myself. I was finally going to have a job and I was finally going to be able to make my own money. I remember I made $1.74 an hour that summer at Taco Bell. I was fourteen years old making $1.74 an hour! I could only work through the summer and up to when school started back up. Then I quit and returned to school. My favorite subjects were math and algebra. I was shy and awkward, and it seemed like I only had friends when I had money!

I always wanted to graduate from Lamar Consolidated High School with my lifelong friends. So, my senior year, I headed back there, but first my grandpa told me "Don't ever hit your parents and stay off the *grass*." Well, I can tell you this, I never hit my parents but I continued smoking the grass. My counselor was Mrs. Krause. She handed me my class schedule. I looked over the schedule and asked her for a schedule change because my classes seemed too hard. But she said, "No, you got this. I believe in you." That really meant a lot to me because I didn't hear that from my family. My biggest dream as a young man was to get that high school diploma because my grandpa and father didn't get to graduate from high school, so I really wanted that diploma. One of my electives was data processing. I took it in hopes of meeting some girls. I was trying desperately to figure out who I was and who I was going to be after school was over.

    I really had no thought past high school about what I wanted to do, but I knew I wanted two things, a job and a girlfriend. So, I knew I had to get that diploma because working at dad's bar was not going to be my future. I was determined to make something of myself. I just was not sure what that meant or even looked like.

4

Enter Rosemary

"He who finds a wife finds a good thing, And obtains favor from the LORD." Proverbs 18:22

My senior year I met my future wife. She was only a freshman, and she was beautiful. When I saw her, I just knew this is my future wife. Her name was Rosemary. I met her at my cousin's house. Her smile lit up a room. I just knew she was the one for me, so I began to pursue her. I even took her to my prom. I wore a tan suit and she wore a light pink dress. My favorite uncle, Manuel, worked at Carpet World and was always giving me money as a young boy. He had a great vibe, cool style, and he had this metal painted '72 Grand Prix that was a sweet ride. He let me drive Rosemary to the prom in it. I was on top of the world. It was such a special night. (He was tragically taken from us to soon. He was murdered at 44. He will always be remembered for his heart of gold) RIP Uncle Manuel.

Rosemary was young, beautiful, and yet shy. Her heart was kind and she carried herself with so much class. Soon it was time for me to graduate. It was also a time in history when Americans were being held hostage in Iran and the government was calling on young men to volunteer for war. I considered it and then said, "Naw, they're gonna need to draft me." I didn't feel like I had what it took to be a soldier. So instead, I took off to California to spend some time with my aunt and uncle and my cousins. All the while, I still kept in touch with Rosemary. I would talk to her on the phone as much as possible.

My uncle was going to get me a job at the Delmonte plant, but when I called home to discuss it with my dad, he said, "No, come back to Rosenberg. They are hiring at the Houston Light & Power for $10.00 an hour." That was a lot of money to me. I knew I wasn't going to get $10 an hour, but I needed to make good money if I wanted my own family. So, I headed back to Rosenberg, Texas. I left on Monday, got back on Tuesday, and started working there on Wednesday morning. I went to the Electric Towers in downtown Houston so I could apply for the job. I applied, interviewed, and got hired the same day. They even asked my dad if he wanted to appy. He said, "No!" My dad and I worked for the same company for 38 ½ years. They saw I took data processing on my transcripts and wanted to test me for that, but I laughed and said, "No, I only took that to meet girls." So, they put me out in the field. My starting pay was $4.55 an hour. From the time I was 18 till I was 57, I worked in the purchasing/logistics department as a material handler until I retired. That was my career. Not only did I work there daily, but I also worked every bit of overtime I could.

One thing is for sure, my grandpa and my dad gave me a very strong work ethic. Maybe too strong. As I grew up, I resented my dad for working so much, but turned right around and put every hour into my career as well. I worked in another town, so I just worked as many hours as I could so I could save up as much money as possible. I worked a lot of hours, but on the weekend, I would come to town and visit my cousins and see Rosemary at the McDonald's where she worked. The minute work was done, I would make that drive. As I drove a blue 360 Honda motorcycle, I could not shake this girl out of my mind. She was my drive to work those long hours and to keep coming back every weekend.

Rosemary's Note To Phillip:

> To: Phillip
> A very sweet and handsome guy. That I love alot and that I always will. And really enjoy being around you.
>
> With Love Always,
> Rosemary Garcia

5

The Great Elope

"And the LORD God said, "It is not good that man should be alone; I will make him a helper comparable to him... And the LORD God caused a deep sleep to fall on Adam, and he slept; and He took one of his ribs, and closed up the flesh in its place. Then the rib which the LORD God had taken from man He made into a woman, and He brought her to the man."
Gen 2:18;21-22

In 1980, Rosemary and I eloped. I was nineteen and she was sixteen. She worked at McDonald's in Rosenberg, Texas, while I worked at the nuclear plant for Houston Lighting & Power. I'd come to her job every weekend. I determined in my heart already that nothing was going to keep me from seeing her. Nothing. I didn't know much about being in a relationship or how to even have one, all I knew was I had to see her every chance I could. This one time, I was on my 360 blue Honda motorcycle when I came to see her. Once she got off work, we just hung out for hours. When it got time for me to leave, she simply wrapped her hands around my neck and said, "Take me with you," in my ear. Without thinking, I just swooped her up on my bike and took off. I ended up bringing her to my apartment in Palacios, Texas. Now I didn't live right down the street, I lived a number of towns over. It started off okay for her, but then it really became difficult for her because I worked so many hours and a ton of overtime. She was always home alone and away from her family and friends. I didn't even consider those things before bringing her back to my apartment. I was just excited to see her whenever I came home from work. Like I said, I loved her and I wanted to be with her and provide for her.

A few months went by and her parents came to the apartment one day. They lived on the west side of Rosenberg. She came from a big family, one of seven kids, the oldest of three girls. She didn't come from a perfect family either. Her parents fought a lot. That's one of the main reasons I believe she was ready to leave home and I think her parents knew that. They also knew she was with me and they trusted me to take care of her. So, on this day, I met her 6'2 cowboy dad. I thought to myself, "Oh God, I'm dead. Hang him high." That's what I expected him to say. But instead, we sat and talked and then they gave me permission to marry her. All of sixteen years old, light-skinned, wavy hair to her shoulders, light brown eyes, and a thin, big smile you could see a block away. My beautiful little Hispanic *west side girlfriend* was now going to be my bride and I was going to be her husband. Neither of us had a clue what that really meant or what to do.

In her parents' house, they were Hispanic Catholics. Her dad was gone a lot because of work. Her mom was home alone with all those kids. Rosemary was the oldest so she did a lot of the laundry, cooking, and chores. Her younger siblings even called her 'mama'. She was a very smart young woman. She decided to get a job at her young age, but because she moved in with me, she didn't even get to graduate high school. She tried three times throughout our marriage in the beginning to finish, but we moved so much for my job. Finally, she just gave up and got a job at Moo Moos Fried Chicken in Palacios, Texas, kind of like an older version of Chick-Fil-A. And when we moved to Bay City, she got a job at Jack In The Box. After that, she got a job at Walmart.

Not only was Rosemary smart and very attractive she was athletic, too. She was very good at sports, especially softball. Coaches were always offering her a chance to come and play for them, but she wanted out of her parents' home and to be as far away as possible from them and their community. She was so easy to talk to and to share with. I loved talking to her and sharing my heart with her. But Rosemary was painfully shy until she had something to say. She knew she didn't want to live at home anymore, but she was by no means ready to be a wife and handle the burdens that come with being home alone as well as trying to meet and fulfill my needs as her new husband. In retrospect, she was still just a child. She didn't know how to express her emotions or to communicate to me how she was feeling but I always felt like she was trying her best to be the best wife she could be.

When we first got married, we would visit Rosenberg, then Bay City for two years, Palacios for two and a half years, and then we moved back to Rosenberg again. Returning to Rosenberg stirred up the hornet's nest. I found out my dad had had an affair on my mom and that he had a son with another woman. I was going through all kinds of emotions: betrayal, anger, depression, and heartbreak. And instead of being there to help mom and to comfort her through all these difficult times, I leaned on my teenage bride to be my emotional support, not knowing that I needed God. I needed a savior that I could reach out to. But instead, I put that pressure on her and when she couldn't give me the support I needed, I started feeling rejected by her. I started feeling like she was drifting away from me and that made me even more angry and frustrated with her. And this also made me want to drink more. Those first six years of our marriage was hard. I worked over forty hours a week, no, more like seventy hours a week. I was addicted to getting that paycheck and to making that money. I was thinking I was providing a good life for us, but I wasn't spending any time building my relationship with my wife.

I thought being a good provider was enough. She was going out with her friends, and I was home drinking. When I wasn't home drinking, I was at work. I started isolating myself and we started to fight more and more. It even became verbally abusive, which I am not proud of at all. In my mind, I felt abandoned by her. How I was feeling gave her more heartache and pressure than she could handle. I was very open about my feelings, but not in a healthy way. I dumped my negativity on her, and she wasn't equipped to handle it or my meltdowns. She was very quiet and reserved about hers. It seemed like she was just a wall and wouldn't let me in. To add insult to injury, during those first six years, Rosemary had three miscarriages, all within in a year and a half. With the third one, she not only lost the child, she lost an ovary as well. I was of no comfort to her. I didn't know how to be. And she was not equipped to tell me how to help her. Yes, I was sad, but I didn't have any idea what she was going through emotionally or physically. She wasn't able to communicate it to me. I'm not sure she ever understood it. She just became more and more distant as time went on, and so, to numb myself from the feeling that she didn't love me, I drank more and more.

After finding out about my dad's affair and having a five-year-old half-brother introduced to me, all I could say to my father was, "Oh, that's cool." I wasn't cool with it at all. It infuriated me. It made me full of rage and hatred. I felt replaced as a son. I felt betrayed. The enemy immediately came to me and whispered in my ear, "See, you were no good. Your father had to have another son from another woman." I also felt betrayed by Rosemary because when I came to her and shared what I learned, she said she had known about the affair for quite some time. Later, I learned she was just trying to protect my heart, but I felt betrayed by her that she kept such a profound secret from me. If she could keep *that secret* from me, what else was she keeping from me? This is how the enemy works. He fills your head with lies, then he gets you to be angry and isolate yourself. I was already so hurt by my parents for abandoning me when I was younger, and now I felt replaced on top of it. I became consumed with my anger and feeling justified for my hatred.

I remember one New Year's Eve, we were having a party. We had a pool table in the living room and had a trailer home that I had owned. It was a two bedroom, and we were up just partying and drinking the night away. This led to a lot of fighting between Rosemary and me. When all the guests left, I cursed her out for going to bed early. What was wrong with me? I let my ego, my pride, my fears, and my pain lead my mouth. She had to work the next day and so did I. The next morning, I went to work hungover. As I was leaving, she said, "That's it," to me. I knew what she meant. It was over. I went to work. I didn't stop and try to say anything to her, I just left. Just me and my ego.

I struggled at work all day. I felt ashamed for how I treated her. I felt lost. And then on my way home that night, while I was riding home on the country roads in a carpool van, I heard the Lord speak to me audibly. He called me by my name. I was just looking out the window thinking to myself, "I blew it. I messed up." Then I heard the audible voice of God say to me, *"Phillip, something beautiful is going to happen in your life and you are going to change for the best."* As soon as I heard the word 'best', I felt my old self leave and the Holy Spirit come in. No more drugs, no more alcohol. I felt like a brand new person. I felt on top of the world. A joy came upon me like I never felt before. "God spoke to me. He knows my name!" As I'm writing this, it's been thirty-six years, and yet, tears are still streaming down my face burning my cheeks. There's just something about when you hear your father's voice *calling your name.* It forever changes you. It lets you know you are loved, you are wanted, and that He's been watching this whole time. And He cares. My experience in that van felt much like the story of Saul on the way to Damascus in *Acts 9:1-9*:

> *"Then Saul, still breathing threats and murder against the disciples of the Lord, went to the high priest and asked letters from him to the synagogues of Damascus, so that if he found any who were of the Way, whether men or women, he might bring them bound to Jerusalem. As he journeyed he came near Damascus, and suddenly a light shone around him from heaven. Then he fell to the ground, and heard a voice saying him, "Saul, Saul, why are you persecuting Me?" And he said, "Who are You, Lord?" Then the Lord said, "I am Jesus, whom you are persecuting. [a]It is hard for you to kick against the goads." So he, trembling and astonished, said, "Lord, what do You want me to do?" Then the Lord said to him, "Arise and go into the city, and you will be told what you must do." And the men who journeyed with him stood speechless, hearing a voice but seeing no one. Then Saul arose from the ground, and when his eyes were opened he saw no one. But they led him by the hand and brought him into Damascus. And he was three days without sight, and neither ate nor drank.*

God's voice does that. It causes you to stop, turn, and go a new way. God's voice allows you to see what He sees, feel what He feels, and know what He thinks of you. Whether He speaks through a song, the word of God, or audibly, trust me, He is speaking to you. Back in 1985, my Aunt Lorene led Rosemary and me to the Lord. She was a "spirit-filled" Catholic and she loved God with all her heart. She was passionate about seeing the loss come to the Lord and she wanted to make sure all her children and all her nieces and nephews knew God and accepted Christ as their savior. Aunt Lorene had planted a seed in our hearts that was now being watered by God. When she led us to God, it didn't change me. That didn't make me desire God. That didn't keep me from drinking and verbally abusing my wife because I still didn't understand that I needed Him. But hearing God in this carpool speak my name out loud, did. It let me know that I did need God, my Father. I couldn't wait to get home and share my experience with Rosemary. I was so excited. I felt brand new! But as soon as I told her, she left me. She grabbed the keys and left the house and didn't look back. I was devastated. I was confused. I said, "God, why isn't she happy for me? God replied, "Phillip, how many times did you say you're sorry before? I answered, "Every weekend." The Lord said, "Then give her a chance to see that you are really changed. This is going to take time."

Like I said, I felt like a brand new person. I couldn't go back to doing things the way I used to do them. Instead, I started going to home studies, Bible studies. I returned to the Catholic Church because it was all I'd ever known. But during mass one Sunday during the Eucharist, I went up to receive the communion and the priest said, "No, you can't "What do you mean I can't?" But God said, "Don't be moved by what you see or hear, but by my word alone."

Thinking Rosemary would be coming back was not my focus after she left. I knew I had hurt her. I was very aware of my hurtful words and actions towards her. I knew I needed to fix me first. I knew my focus needed to be on God. Soon after, we separated. I later found out that she had started seeing someone six weeks prior to getting separated from me. This explained her distancing herself from me. This explained why when I told her about my carpool experience, it caused her to flee. But I wasn't angry. I felt a peace and calm come over me once again and I just began to pray for her silently. God was teaching me His ways. I was learning how to walk out grace and mercy.

   I would go to church and I would feel like I wanted more and more and more and more of God. As the days went on, my Aunt Lorene told me about a church called Living Waters that had a prayer house where the men gathered to pray on Thursdays. She told me I should go there and get prayer. When I arrived there, men were speaking in tongues and praying. "What's this?" I thought. A gift of tongues. "What is that?" I couldn't even walk inside. I just stood still at the doorway; I couldn't even walk in. I just saw men kneeling and praying. And the spirit overtook me right then. It flooded me on the inside and I began to weep uncontrollably like a dam bursting. I began to purge all the pain that was in my heart. It was like a flood that was pouring out of me. The Holy Spirit was doing the work. The men left me alone and I purged my soul, my heart, my cares. After some time passed, a large, burly man named Victor Duran came to me and boldly said to me, "Jesus wants to know if you want to receive the baptism of the Holy Spirit with the evidence of speaking in tongues?" I nodded and asked, "What do I have to do?" He pointed to a chair and said, "Sit in this chair and we will lay hands on you." But before they could even touch me, the Holy Spirit filled me! I mean it. I sat in the chair and I had my gift, the outpouring of tongues. God was so good to me. "God, I want all the gifts you have for me," I said under my breath. "God, come be my father and teach me how to live, how to love, and how to serve you, God. Show me how to love like you love. Teach me how to be a man in your image."

Every time I had a problem from that day forward, I would just stop and ask, "Jesus, what would you do in this situation when you walked on this earth?" I talked to Him man to man. I saw Him as my answer and my wise counsel. When He'd answer me, I'd just go do it. Whatever it was, I just did it, no questions asked. It didn't matter what I heard or saw around me, I stood on my word and I stood on the audible voice of the Lord. Soon, I started attending Church of Living Waters regularly. I attended every meeting I could. One Sunday in particular, Pastor Gene Franks of Church Of Living Waters was preaching on Lazarus being raised from the dead and becoming a new man in John 11:1-44:

> "Now a certain man was sick, Lazarus of Bethany, the town of Mary and her sister Martha. 2 It was that Mary who anointed the Lord with fragrant oil and wiped His feet with her hair, whose brother Lazarus sick. Therefore the sisters sent to Him, saying, "Lord, behold, he whom You love is sick." When Jesus heard that, He said, "This sickness is not unto death, but for the glory of God, that the Son of God may be glorified through it." Now Jesus loved Martha and her sister and Lazarus. So, when He heard that he was sick, He stayed two more days in the place where He was. Then after this He said to the disciples, "Let us go to Judea again." The disciples said to Him, "Rabbi, lately the Jews sought to stone You, and are You going there again?" Jesus answered, "Are there not twelve hours in the day? If anyone
> walks in the day, he does not stumble, because he sees the light of this world. But if one walks in the night, he

stumbles, because the light is not in him." These things He said, and after that He said to them, "Our friend Lazarus sleeps, but I go that I may wake him up." Then His disciples said, "Lord, if he sleeps he will get well." However, Jesus spoke of his death, but they thought that He was speaking about taking rest in sleep. Then Jesus said to them plainly, "Lazarus is dead. And I am glad for your sakes that I was not there, that you may believe. Nevertheless let us go to him." Then Thomas, who is called the Twin, said to his fellow disciples, "Let us also go, that we may die with Him."

So when Jesus came, He found that he had already been in the tomb four days. Now Bethany was near Jerusalem, about two miles away. And many of the Jews had joined the women around Martha and Mary, to comfort them concerning their brother. Then Martha, as soon as she heard that Jesus was coming, went and met Him, but Mary was sitting in the house. Now Martha said to Jesus, "Lord, if You had been here, my brother would not have died. But even now I know that whatever You ask of God, God will give You." Jesus said to her, "Your brother will rise again." Martha said to Him, "I know that he will rise again in the resurrection at the last day." Jesus said to her, "I am the resurrection and the life. He who believes in Me, though he may die, he shall live. And whoever lives and believes in Me shall never die. Do you believe this?" She said to Him, "Yes, Lord, I believe that You are the Christ, the Son of God, who is to come into the world." And when she had said these things, she went her way and secretly called Mary her sister, saying, "The Teacher has come and is calling for you." As soon as she heard that, she arose quickly and came to Him. Now Jesus had not yet come into the town, but was in the place where Martha met Him. Then the Jews who were with her in the house, and comforting her, when they saw that Mary rose up quickly and went out, followed her,]saying, "She is going to the tomb to weep there." Then, when Mary came where Jesus was, and saw Him, she fell down at His feet, saying to Him, "Lord, if You had been here, my brother would not have died." Therefore, when Jesus saw her weeping, and the Jews who came with her weeping, He groaned in the spirit and was troubled. And He said, "Where have you laid him?" They said to Him, "Lord, come and see." Jesus wept. Then the Jews said, "See how He loved him!" And some of them said, "Could not this Man, who opened the eyes of the blind, also have kept this man from dying?" Then Jesus, again groaning in Himself, came to the tomb. It was a cave, and a stone lay against it. Jesus said, "Take away the stone." Martha, the sister of him who was dead, said to Him, "Lord, by this time there is a stench, for he has been dead four days." Jesus said to her, "Did I not say to you that if you would believe you would see the glory of God?" Then they took away the stone from the place where the dead man was lying. And Jesus lifted up His eyes and said, "Father, I thank You that You have heard Me. And I know that You always hear Me, but because of the people who are standing by I said this, that they may believe that You sent Me." Now when He had said these things, He cried with a loud voice, "Lazarus, come forth!" And he who had died came out bound hand and foot with graveclothes, and his face was wrapped with a cloth. Jesus said to them, "Loose him, and let him go." Then many of the Jews who had come to Mary, and had seen the things Jesus did, believed in Him."

I wanted to be a new man, so I listened for what came next. I was willing to do whatever God asked me to do. So, Pastor Gene said, "Take off your grave clothes!" I was wearing gray clothes, so I thought he said, "Take off your gray clothes." LOL, I thought, "Oh Lord, do I really have to take off my clothes?" But then Pastor Jean repeated himself and said, "Take off your *grave* clothes. You are no longer dead. Take off your grave clothes." I said, "Oh, thank God. Thank you, God, for opening my ears to hear the truth so that I did not take off my gray clothes in the middle of this service." It's ok, God has a sense of humor. God knew my heart was just so pure and ready to obey.

Going to church six days a week and going to home Bible studies and prayer at the prayer house didn't seem to fill me up. I had such a hunger. I wanted to know more about God. I wanted to understand who I was in God, so I read my word more, went to more Bible studies, and prayed and spoke in tongues as often as I could. One of my favorite verses at that time was:

> *"Ask, and it will be given to you; seek, and you will find; knock, and it will be opened to you. For everyone who asks receives, and he who seeks finds, and to him who knocks it*
> *will be opened." Mt 7:7-8*

I also learned it wasn't enough to just hear the word, I had to *apply the word* in every area of my life in order for my life to change. For my mindset to be new, I learned that it was more important to be obedient than to sacrifice. So, I stood on that word and learned humility:

> *"Has the Lord as great delight in burnt*
> *offerings and sacrifices,*
> *As in obeying the voice of the Lord?*
> *Behold, to obey is better than sacrifice,*
> *And to heed than the fat of rams.*
> *1 Sam 15:22*

I chose obedience.

I also learned how to truly forgive. To move forward, the Holy Spirit told me *I have to forgive*. Holy Spirit came in and the old me came out. God had to blind Saul so he could see, but God had to take the blinders off me so that I could see. God is such a good God, such a loving father. He meets each of us where we are at.

> "For by grace you have been saved, washed through faith." Ephesians 2:8

> "For I will forgive their wickedness and will remember their sin no more." Hebrews 8:12

6

Growing Pains

"For the love of Christ compels us, because we judge thus: that if One died for all, then all died; and He died for all, that those who live should live no longer for themselves, but for Him who died for them and rose again.: 2 Cor 5: 14-15

When I think back to all the things that happened between Rosemary and me, getting back together took a lot of selflessness and putting someone else's needs before your own without the hope or the guarantee that we would reunite. I just wanted to love her the way God loved me. I wanted her to know that the love of God was real. God did that in me. He helped me to see her how He sees her. I remember once I tried to take her out to dinner. I just wanted to talk to her. I just wanted to be in her company. We were still separated at the time, but at the last minute, she canceled on me because a family member of the person she was seeing at the time had found a tumor. This is what she told me on the phone. And instead of getting mad, The

Holy Spirit came over me and I said, "Okay." I chose right then that I'm going to be real with God the way God's been real with me. So instead of getting frustrated or being in my flesh or being discouraged, I began to pray for this person. I began praying for the healing. I prayed that they would no longer be able to see that tumor in the head anymore. Weeks later, I was visiting Rosemary and she just out of the blue said to me, "Oh, you remember the person that had the tumor?" I said, "Yeah." She said, "Well, it's gone. When they went back to do another MRI, they couldn't find it." The goodness of God.

God is always answering our prayers. He's always listening to us and He is also changing us. I prayed every day for Rosemary that even if she doesn't come back to me, I want her to know you the way I know you, Lord. Don't let anyone else hurt her again the way I did. Lord, give her someone who will treat her like a queen and love her the same as you do me. These are the words I would say over and over in my prayers at night. We didn't have children and we didn't even have a future (so it seemed in the natural) because we had done so much to each other, but God had different plans for us. But first, he just had to get us in the right mindset. He needed us to die to ourselves and our old beliefs and learn His heart and His will. God's love covers a multitude of sin. God doesn't do the punishing; He does the reconciliation and the restoration *if* you will humble yourself before Him. Forgiving seems hard, but through Jesus, you can do it!

"Love suffers long and is kind; love does not envy; love does not parade itself, is not puffed up; does not behave

PS: I Love You

rudely, does not seek its own, is not provoked, thinks no evil; does not rejoice in iniquity, but rejoices in the truth; bears all things, believes all things, hopes all things, endures all things. Love never fails."
1 Corinthians 13:4-8

"And above all things have fervent love for one another, for "love will cover a multitude of sins." 1 Peter 4:8

I never let the enemy use my insecurity or pain to hurt her or remind her of the past. I didn't allow the enemy to use our current situation or the other gentleman in her life to cause me to be frustrated, angry, or even jealous. Instead, it just motivated me to press in with Him. I chose to be with the Lord and to be all in with God so that I could have a better life. A life pleasing to Him because He first loved me, died for me, and his love, despite all my flaws, loved me the same. Pastor Gene said it best when he said, "Don't go picking at the scab because you don't know how long it will take to heal." I chose to walk in my healing. But don't get me wrong, the enemy would try to pick at it for me. I had to choose to take my own thoughts captive.

"But if the unbeliever leaves, let it be so. The brother or the sister is not bound in such circumstances; God has called us to live in peace." 1 Corinthians 7:15

7

My Road to Damascus

"As he journeyed he came near Damascus, and suddenly a light shone around him from heaven. Then he fell to the ground, and heard a voice saying to him, "Saul, Saul, why are you persecuting Me?"
And he said, "Who are You, Lord?" Then the Lord said, "I am Jesus, whom you are persecuting. [a]It is hard for you to kick against the goads." So he, trembling and astonished, said, "Lord, what do You want me to do?" Then the Lord said to him, "Arise and go into the city, and you will be told what you must do." Acts 9:3-6

I went to hear God's word six days a week. I was getting divorced and I was learning about forgiveness and what it truly meant to forgive. The scripture that always stuck with me was "forgive others so you can be forgiven."

"Do not repay anyone evil for evil. Be careful to do what is right in the eyes of everyone." Romans 12:17

In order to move forward and continue to grow, I had to forgive so I could be forgiven. As soon as I said, "Lord, I forgive Rosemary," I felt a switch turn on. And almost instantaneously, my heart was full of love again for her. It was as if nothing had ever happened. I was reminded of what God had told me in that carpool van, "Phillip, something beautiful is going to happen in your life and you are going to change for the best." We are going to have a change for the best once that old me comes out and the Holy Spirit comes in and dwells in me, just like Saul. As I came down that city road, I started off one way, but I ended up changed.

We are not capable of such change in and of ourselves. Only through God can we absolutely become a new man. When Saul was on his way to Damascus, he was one way. But when God got a hold of him, He blinded him so that he could see. That was the same for me. I was blind, blind with rage, blind with frustration, blind with selfishness. I was just blind. I had been fed a bunch of lies by the devil and I believed them. See, the devil started at me at a young age. He never wanted me to know who I really was in God and he did everything in his power to make me feel unloved, unwanted, unworthy. It was all lies. And when God showed up that night on that road while I was in that carpool van, all those lies came to a halt. It was time for me to know that I was loved, I was wanted, I was created for a purpose, and God alone would change my heart. That's not to say that I never struggled with these things, but now I had a savior to help me. I was no longer going to need Rosemary to fill my void or take my pain. That was never her job. That work was done on the cross by Jesus.

That's when I finally realized I blew it with Rosemary. So, I turned my heart towards praying for her. I decided I wanted her to be happy. I wanted her to know love and I wanted her to have a great life. That's the difference between a selfish love and a God-fearing love for someone. You want the very best for them even if that doesn't include you. I would pray every night, "Lord, I don't care if she never comes back to me again, but I pray that she knows you like I know you. I pray that she will find a husband that will love her and treat her like a queen. So, I put her in your hands, Lord! And wherever she's at, touch her right where she's at."

At this point, I started serving in the church. I was going to church regularly; I was serving to the best of my ability; and I was growing in God. I had taken my eyes off of me and started taking care of others. I started becoming a family at the church. I started learning how it was to care about other people more than you care about yourself. I was learning to be humble. I was learning to be selfless. I was learning to love the unlovable. Then one day, Rosemary contacted me and asked if she could come to church with me. I agreed to pick her up. But as I was waiting for her in the car, she came down the apartment stairs and said, "Something came up and I'm not going to be able to go." A few weeks later, she said, "Okay, I'm ready to go to church with you," but on Sunday, she came down the stairs and said, "Phillip, something else came up." The third time she called and said, "I want to go to church with you." I told her, "Look, Rosemary, by the time I get to your apartment you're going to be invited to go somewhere else. Something is always going to get in the way of you going to church. You're going to have to decide if you want to go to church or not." She said, "Come get me. I'm going to church." I said, "Okay, be ready. I'll pick you up at 10:15am." Service started at 10:30 back then. Sure enough, like clockwork, she came down the stairs laughing and saying, "Phillip, you're right. But this time she says, "I was invited to go somewhere else, but I chose not to go because I have a date with Jesus." As she said this to me, tears welled up and streamed down my face. I said, "Oh God, I know you have your daughter in the palm of your hand. Thank you, God, for loving her the same."

So, I picked her up and took her to church. We sat in the back row. At the end of service, Pastor Gene would say, "Every head bow and every eye closed. Whoever wants to accept Jesus Christ as their Lord and Savior raise your hand. called for salvation it came time to close our eyes so that they could ask those who had not accepted Christ yet to come up and receive Christ, I glanced over at Rosemary to see if she raised her hand, but she didn't. So, I got discouraged. I said, "God, she's your daughter. I know you love her the same." Next thing I know, I see her walking down the aisle. After church, I offered to take her to get a bite to eat. "Let's go get some lunch, I'm hungry," I said. She was happy to go. She was so happy sitting at the table. I said, "Hey, why are you so happy? She said, "I'm happy because God loves me. I raised my hand today and Jesus came into my heart. I felt forgiven. I felt loved." See, God does honor our heart's desires. He whispered in my ear in that moment and said, "See, Phillip, you don't have to see what I'm doing; you just have to believe."

> *"Therefore, if anyone is in Christ, he is a new creation; old things have passed away; behold, all things have become new."*
> 2 Corinthians 5:17

I love how God teaches us. He never condemns me, but to show me His love, he convicts me, and it causes my heart to change. That's when the change happens.

After a few months, Rosemary was still coming to church with me. One Sunday, I saw that she wanted to go up to the altar. Later she said, "Phillip, not only has God forgive me, but now I have forgiven myself." She would later teach others this very same principle.

8

New Wine Skin

"And no one puts new wine into old wineskins; or else the new wine bursts the wineskins, the wine is spilled, and the wineskins are ruined. But new wine must be put into new wineskins." Mark 2:22

What is the purpose for me being here? I don't know how to feel or how to think about anything during this time. I thought I was a nobody even as a kid. When my parents would whip me when I was younger, I would think to myself, "Why am I here? Nobody loves me." But God says in John 8:32:

"Then you will know the truth, and the truth will set you free." John 8:32

The truth is I am a child of God. Children are a gift from God. This gave me hope to strive for a better life. You have to learn to distinguish between Satan's voice and the voice of God. The voice of God rings with truth. The devil takes a little truth and mixes it with a great big lie. It won't match what the word of God says. It'll match a portion of it or sound like something from the Bible, but it won't be the living Word of God. God is truth.

> *"God is not human, that he should lie,*
> *not a human being, that he should change his mind.*
> *Does he speak and then not act?*
> *Does he promise and not fulfill?"*
> *Num 23:19*

God brings peace, restoration, hope, and encouragement. The enemy will come dressed like light, but he doesn't leave light. When he leaves, he leaves a mess. He leaves pain, suffrage, hurt, confusion, and chaos. The enemy is trying to rob you so that you never know God, never know the promises of God, and never get to see the promises of God fulfilled in your life.

> *"The thief comes only to steal and kill and destroy; I*
> *have come that they may have life and have it to the full."*
> *John 10:10*

God wants to love you God wants you to know your wanted God wants you to have revelation.

It's been really hard for me to trust people. I have to lean a lot to God. I had to learn from God how to trust Him and how to trust the Holy Spirit so that I could live a peaceful life. He taught me not to change who He made me to be for somebody else. He wanted me to know who I am in Him and who He is to me. Even those of us who are saved can say things that are not the truth. Even those of us who have good intentions can hurt one another without meaning to. So, it's important that you ask God what He thinks about a matter. I have to ask God, "What do you think," or "How do you see this situation, God?" daily. The enemy comes to steal, kill, and destroy. I made it a point to say he may come to steal, kill, and destroy, but he isn't going to use my mouth to do it. I took my thoughts captive and learned 'not to lean on my own understanding but every word of the Lord.'

> *"Trust in the Lord with all your heart*
> *and lean not on your own understanding;*
> *in all your ways submit to him,*
> *and he will make your paths straight. "*
> *Proverbs 3:5-6*

I cried out to God and you can cry out to God, too. Just say, "God, I want every good and perfect gift. I want to be able to walk on this earth in peace. I want to be able to proclaim your word. I want to have an abundance. I want to have the victory. God, I want to do things your way." When you say this and surrender yourself to God and let go of pride, there is nothing that you can't do. There is nothing that you can't have because *God will make a way*. He may have to prune you first, but He will always make sure that you have everything that you need. I'm not saying you're never going to have problems. I had problems even with

Rosemary and I's new marriage. There were battles, but I would not fight her. I would ask God to show me the truth and *teach me how to love her.* Teach me how to lead her. Teach me how to respond. Teach me how to communicate with her. As I was growing my faith, I was also learning how to walk in my power and authority, and so was Rosemary.

I soon learned what it means to take it one day at a time. Grace and mercy are new each day. I vowed not to lean on the way I think things should go or contemplate why things are happening in a certain way. I just leaned on God. The difference here is the difference between religion and relationship. God doesn't do it the same way every time. God treats people as individuals. God treats us according to our heart. God treats us according to his perfect will. There is no 'fair' with God. God has more than enough for everyone. We are not to have our eyes on each other; we are to have our eyes on God. It is God who gives us what we need and what we want. Even when I was trying to win my wife back, I couldn't have done it in and of myself. I had to wait on God. He needed to heal her. She needed to feel loved by God and she needed to be set free like me. I would have had no way of knowing if she was set free because only God can judge the heart. My only job was to put her in His hands and trust in Him. I tried to do what God in me in her, but it doesn't work that way.

God said to me one day, "Are you finished?" I started to laugh. He knew my heart. I said, "Yes, Lord, I'm finished. Lord, forgive me. I commit her to you and to your hands.

Your will be done." She told me later after we remarried that when she used to go to the clubs with her friends, she had no peace, and she didn't feel good while she was there. After she told me this, I remember crying out to God and telling him, "Thank you, Lord. I had no idea you were answering my prayers. I know now I cannot trust in what I can see; I have to have faith that you do hear me and that you are answering me. I kept on putting my trust in God and studying my word. I decided to be all in with God no matter what.

    We are all called to forgive. But it doesn't mean that your relationships or marriages will be restored. That will happen only if God says so. If He says it will happen, you can bet it will happen because God can touch anyone's heart. God can heal anyone's wounds, just surrender your will and surrender them to God. Sometimes you have to love people even if you have no way of knowing if they will ever love you back. This is what it means to walk in the fullness of God and to love them the same. My mom was an alcoholic. My Aunt Lorene, a spirit-filled Catholic, said to me, "I always wanted my sister to get set free. Little did I know that by leading you to the Lord, my nephew, and by you getting saved first, then your mom would come to the Lord." This is how God works behind the scenes. God has the right order; we don't. We just have to be obedient.

> *"Truly you are a God who has been hiding himself,*
> *the God and Savior of Israel."*
> Isaiah 45:15

I just want to take this time to tell you if you have been pouring out your heart to God and you've been praying and asking God for things, just trust and believe and know He hears you. He hears your heart, and he is behind the scenes working it out. It doesn't matter how long it takes; God will work it out. As I was going through the wilderness, when I was seemingly a basket case, he found me and called me by name. God knows us before we ever know Him, and He wants nothing more than to be in a relationship with you. He loves you the same, right here, right now. Whether you're at your lowest or your highest, His arms are wide open ready to receive you.

    Even though Rosemary was changed, and we were both different people, she was still soft spoken and didn't speak a lot. But when she did, wow!, amazing revelation came out of her. She was a mighty warrior for God and she loved to pray for me and my family. This is one of the many ways she showed us her love. She showed her love in actions, not empty promises or words. Sometimes, the simple gesture of putting her arm around my shoulder would show me how much she loved me. Trust me, for years I didn't understand that that is what I was experiencing. I would get so frustrated, I would sit in my car and cry and say, "God, I don't want to leave, but I need you." I would drive around the block or go to the park and just walk around. I would speak to God until I felt better. Then I would go home. When I got home, all I wanted was to hear, "I love you." All I wanted was that warm embrace. I needed to learn how to receive love from my wife the way she knew how to show it. I needed to learn how to be patient.

One afternoon I heard a knock at the door. It was Rosemary. She said she wanted to come home, but something inside me would not say yes. Instead, I told her, "Rosemary, I just can't, not because I don't want to. I just can't go back and forth. I love you too much. It would hurt me too much. Yes, I want you to come home, but I can't be a yo-yo right now. You only want to come home because it's hard where you're at, but I need you to want to come home for good." She shook her head. She understood and she left. I began to weep to the Lord, "God, I'm so sorry. I hope that was you. I felt like that was you." The Lord said, "Okay, are you finished?" I said, "Yes, Lord, I'm done." Then God began the process of healing our marriage.

All I had ever wanted to hear was "I love you," but what is that? What is love? Is it the word or is it the actions? After all, God did in Rosemary, myself, and in our life together, I finally realized that she really does love me. God said, "Look across the table." As I sit here remembering our life together, I'm looking at a picture of us in a heart-shaped frame and it says, *"PS, I Love You."* Why is this so hard to believe someone could really love me?

Even after God healed our relationship and put us back together, we still had to walk through a lot of things together. The Lord was merciful to us both. It was still hard for Rosemary in the beginning to speak to me about her feelings or what she was going through because of her past shame and hurts. I would tell her many times, "Mama, tell me what's going on so I know how to pray for you." I would encourage her to open up to me. Sometimes she could and sometimes she couldn't. When she couldn't, it would open up fear for me again. I began to doubt that we were going to make it. But that was a lie. I was loved not just by her, but by God. I have to trust the process and believe I am loved just the same.

9

The White Dress

*"And His garments became radiant and exceedingly
white, as no launderer on earth can whiten them."
Mark 9:3*

God said, "Okay, now you can ask Rosemary again to be your wife." So, I did, and she said, "Yes!" Rosemary wore a white wedding dress, and boy, did people have a lot to say about that. People have a lot of opinions about a lot of things, but we knew why she was wearing a white dress. So, when someone asked me, "Hey, why is Rosemary wearing a white dress? You've already been married before." I simply smiled and said, "Because she's washed white as snow." Rosemary is washed by the blood of the Lamb. A new creation in Christ Jesus.

*"Come now, let us settle the matter,"
says the Lord. "Though your sins are like scarlet,
they shall be as white as snow; though they are red
as crimson they shall be like wool." Isaiah 1:18*

This time would be different. No justice of the peace for my Rosemary. We rented the civic center and Pastor Gene from our church was the man that was going to marry us. The day of the wedding, it poured cats and dogs. It was raining so hard, my father-in-law was stuck inside his car. Everybody was frantically moving around saying, "Hey, we should cancel this wedding." I said, "Oh no, I'm marrying her today. I'm marrying Rosemary and today she's going to be my wife." We had to move things around, but that's okay because God makes all things work together for our good, even in the rain. Truly, it was a new beginning for Rosemary and me. The rain was just another sign of us being washed.

> *"Yet you desired faithfulness even in the womb;*
> *you taught me wisdom in that secret place.*
> *Cleanse me with hyssop, and I will be clean;*
> *wash me, and I will be whiter than snow."*
> Psalm 51:6-7

That day, we said our vows before God, our pastor, and our family. God put us together again even better than we were before. Rosemary was my gift from God. She was the tangible love of God to me. She was my rib. She did so much for me, and yet still, the enemy would taunt me and tell me she didn't care. From time to time, I couldn't always see it. I couldn't always feel it. Sometimes I would sit in my car saying, "God, I'm getting the urge to leave again. I'm hurting and I need you." I'd drive around the block until God would come and bring me peace. And then I would go back home to my Rosemary. I was learning how to sacrifice for my wife.

    As a leader, you got to show up, make sacrifices, and make the choice to stick it out even when things get hard. I had to learn that life is not always fair. It's not always going to go your way. I also had to learn that there's an enemy out there that would love for me to give in, give up, or move on, but because God was so good to me and because He restored my marriage to Rosemary, I was willing to make those sacrifices. I was willing to keep showing up and doing what I needed to do. The enemy was always trying to resurrect the old man. He was always trying to destroy the new man in me by planting reminders of what Rosemary had done before or reminders of what my parents didn't do for me as a child. The enemy was always trying to make me think I was unloved, unwanted, or that I was somehow not good enough. This is the trick of the enemy. The word says, "He comes to steal, kill, and destroy." So be ready for the fight. Do not allow the enemy to steal your identity in Christ. As a leader, you have to fight fire with fire. You don't wrestle flesh and blood; you wrestle against powers and principalities in high places.

> *"For our struggle is not against flesh and blood, but against the rulers, against the authorities, against the powers of this dark world and against the spiritual forces of evil in the heavenly realms." Eph 6:12*

You cry out to God and God listens. God gives you the strategies. God gives you the wisdom. God loves on you. And God will give you back your peace. But it's a choice. You have to choose God every day. You choose Jesus as your savior every single day. You have to choose the Holy Spirit every day. And you have to choose to let that old man stay dead every day. For example, in my home, we used to do drugs. We'd drink on the weekends and have parties with friends over, things like that. But even then, when I first gave my heart to the Lord and I was so on fire and so in love with God, the enemy would have someone show up at my house with alcohol or drugs. Me, I was not even drinking alcohol, I was drinking soda, yet someone would bring drugs and line them up on the dining table. I had to say no. I'm sorry I don't do these kinds of things in my life; I don't do this at all.

Another time, this gentleman put lines on my kitchen counter, and I said, "Nope, not going to do it." God showed up in that moment. I was so proud of myself. But God used it as a teaching moment and said to me, "You said this is how you used to be when your wife would be trying to sleep." And I said, "Oh Lord, I told all these old friends I gave my heart to Jesus. I don't drink anymore." Those people stopped coming around. I couldn't go back to my old friends and my old lifestyle if I was going to stay a new man. I had to live my new life with my new friends. The enemy was always trying to get me to go back to being that old man. I remember before I knew Christ, I would just get drunk and cry out for help. I'd put a rifle to my head just to get Rosemary's attention. I just wanted Rosemary to take away the rifle, hug me!, and tell me she loves me! And she did that every time. Now, if the rifle would have gone off, it would have been considered suicide, but my intentions were never to kill myself. I just wanted to know that I was loved. But that wasn't the case anymore. I wasn't going to cause that trauma to my wife nor was I going to allow that trauma to come near me anymore. I would remind that trauma and those bad memories, "Hey, you don't live here anymore. Jesus Christ lives in me now. And My God does love me. He loves me the same every minute of every day.

> *"Therefore, if anyone is in Christ, the new creation has come: The old has gone, the new is here!"*
> 2 Corinthians 5:17

"Go back to drinking now, it's okay, you're alone now. Rosemary's gone." That's another conniving trick that the devil tried to use to get me to start drinking again. He would try to come in while I was in morning prayer and wouldn't stop until I went to bed that night.

> *"As a dog returns to its vomit, so fools repeat their folly."* Prv 26:11

See, the devil, he's always a liar and he always comes in like he has wisdom to speak, but he doesn't know how to speak the truth. He only knows how to lie. My trust is in the Lord. I said, "No, devil, I'm not going back to drinking. I'm going to continue to serve in our house; I'm going to continue to serve in our church; and I'm going to continue to serve God.

I am not going to change who I am just because my life circumstances may change. I have put away the old wineskin and I'm putting on my new wineskin and following Jesus." Just then, I heard God whisper to me, "Remember, before your children, before your wife, it was you and I." Amen.

> "Yet I hold this against you: You have forsaken the love you had at first." Rev 2:4

Before there was me and Rosemary, there was me and God. Before there were children, there was me and God. I will continue to serve God.

    We serve a personal God. We serve a God that's so personal that he allowed his son to come and be born in the flesh. God became flesh for us, so he knows how we feel. He feels everything we feel. He, Jesus, born of the virgin Mary, suffered on the cross for each of us. So, all I had to do was ask God and He always showed up. God would always answer my questions and show me the errors of my ways. Anytime God showed me things from how I showed up in my marriage the first time, I would go and repent to Rosemary. I would let her know that I wasn't that person anymore. This helped me to fall more in love with her and helped her to know I was truly a different man.

> "Beware of the false prophets, who come to you in sheep's clothing, but inwardly are ravenous wolves. You will know them by their fruits." Matthew 7:15-16

It doesn't happen all in one day and you can't just make it happen. It's not one time. You have to choose that you're going to be different in your heart and that you're going to make new decisions and new choices. You're going to have to choose to do the right thing every single day. You must choose to walk in integrity whether you get the girl, the job, the promotion, or the title. None of it really matters. What does matter is that you've given your heart to the Lord and laid down your old life (self). You are a new man. In order for Christ to be living in you, you have to walk that out every day.

How do you know if you are living by the fruits of the spirit?

> "But the fruit of the Spirit is love, joy, peace, forbearance, kindness, goodness, faithfulness, 23 gentleness and self-control. Against such things there is no law." Gal 5:22-23

The enemy was constantly trying to mock me and make me feel like I was an idiot for getting back together with her. They would always try to remind me of her indiscretions from our first marriage, but we were both new creatures in Christ Jesus and I chose to take my thoughts captive. I chose to stand on the word, and I chose not to listen to the voice of the enemy. When I tried to get Rosemary to speak, I did a lot of things to her that caused her drama. I had to remember that I had a part in it as well. During our first marriage, every time I didn't feel loved, or I didn't feel worthy, I was the one who chose to drink. I was the one who chose to put the rifle to my head and demand her to tell me that she loved me. I had to remember that it was my responsibility to get my love from God until I could love my wife for who she was and not put any false expectations on her. I had to truly trust in God for this healing process.

Photo Album

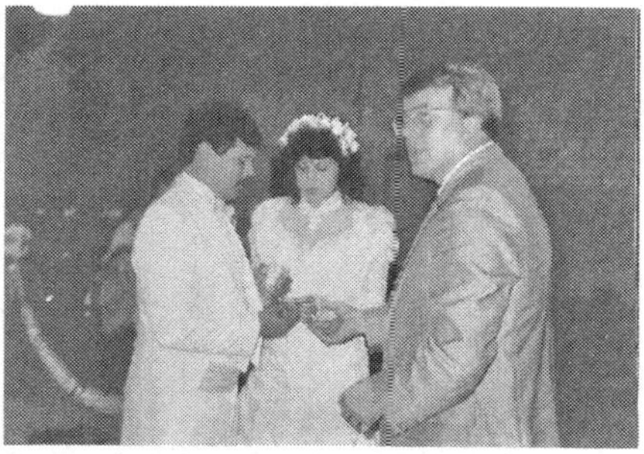

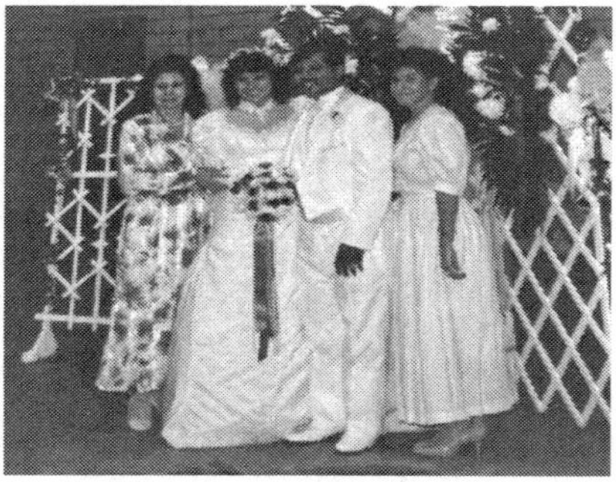

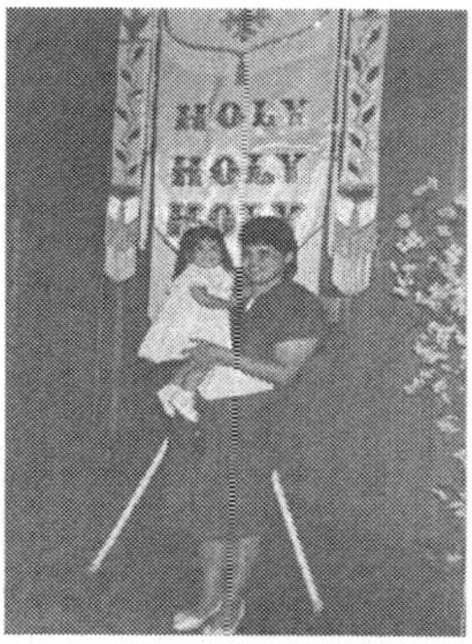
HOLY
HOLY

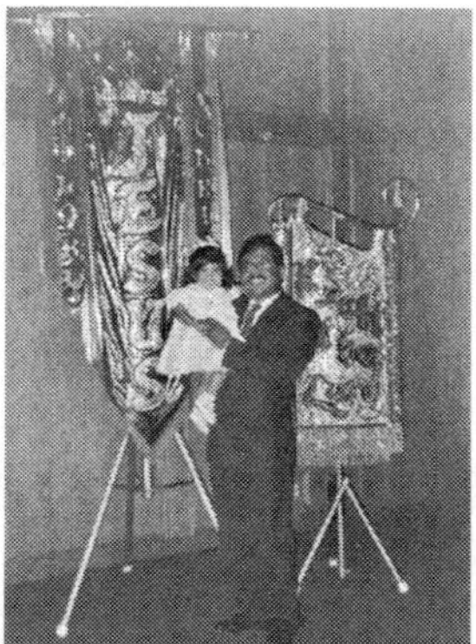

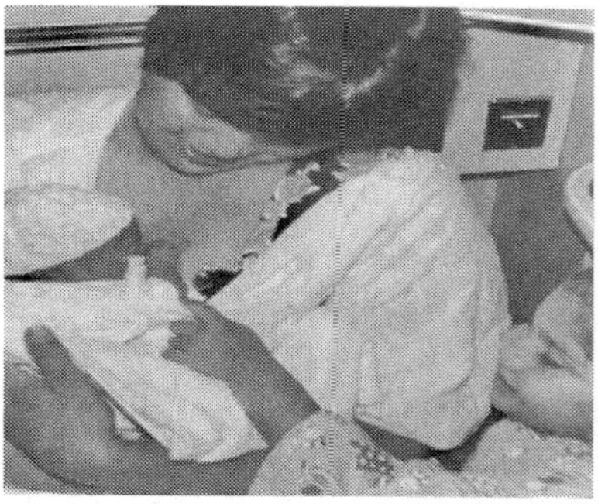

PS: I Love You

10

Miracles Can And Will Happen

"God is not a man, that He should lie, Nor a son of man, that He should repent. Has He said, and will He not do? Or has He spoken, and will He not make it good?" Num 23:19

Here we are, married again, loving ourselves, and learning to love one another. We're learning to heal and to trust all over again. We're serving in church and learning how to hear the voice of the Lord, and then Rosemary got pregnant again. We were so excited. She had already lost one ovary and three prior miscarriages, so it was extremely important to us that she be able to keep this baby. We had just moved our trailer home to a new acre of land that we purchased when she went to the restroom in the middle of the night and there was blood in the toilet. We thought it was the baby. I scooped it up, got her dressed, and took her to the hospital at 3:00 a.m. to be checked out. She was okay, but she needed rest and liquids. I went home and get her some soups, but I was so delirious and not sure what I was supposed to do. Thank God the nurse encouraged me to go home and get somethings in order. Rosemary was about a month pregnant at this point. When I came back, she was gone. I saw a nurse and I just stood there looking at the empty bed confused. The nurse who was a godly woman said, "Was it your wife?" I said, "Yes, ma'am." She said, "She's okay, but they're having to give her a hysterectomy because we couldn't stop the bleeding, but I'm praying for her." She must've saw the shocked look on my face because then she said, "I've seen you all here before. You guys are wanting children, correct? I said, "Yes, ma'am." She said, "Well, it's time to pray." I called my mother-in-law and caught her up with everything that was happening with Rosemary.

After I hung up with my mother-in-law, I looked out the third-floor window and I just started staring at a dumpster. I just go so angry. No, truth be told, I got angry with God. "God, why? Why can't we have a baby? Why can't we keep a baby? There are people that have babies every day and throw them in dumpsters. All we want is our promise. All we want is our children that are for us." The next thing I know, the Holy Spirit said, "Keep trusting in me." A peace fell on me and I took a deep breath. And the next thing I know, a young doctor came out and said, "She's okay. We found the problem. It's not her ovary, so you can try again in six weeks." Rosemary did lose the baby that day.

A few weeks later was, Mother's Day rolled around. This was always a hard day for Rosemary. I just saw a stream of tears rolling down her face as we sat in church and all I could do was just reach my hand out and touch hers. She came from such a large family. She didn't want a huge family, but she did want children. I always wanted six children. By this point, we had four in heaven. I would tell Rosemary, "Mama, it's okay, we have four babies in heaven and one day when we get there, those babies are going to pull on your dress and introduce themselves to you. So yuou can celebrate Mother's Day, it's going to be okay." We cried together and continued to pray to God and stand on our word trusting and believing for the impossible because *"everything is possible through Christ who gives us our strength."* We would take walks at night and talk about what God was doing.

Then Came April

And finally, in March of 1990, my daughter, April Lynn, was born. The day Rosemary went into labor, I remember being so excited for the baby coming. We had been walking the weeks leading up to the delivery. We walked a lot. Rosemary and I would walk around the block and talk about the things we were going to do with our children and the life that we wanted. The other times we just talked about the goodness of God and what He has done for us. Then when the time came, she just looked to me and said, "It's time, Phillip." I took her to the hospital but there were complications, so they had to do an emergency C-section. The doctor, Dr. Sandals, who was taking good care of Rosemary, spoke life over her and the baby and said, "You are going to have this child. I remember you two and I remember I told you that you would get pregnant and have a baby, and I'm here to tell you, you will have this child." I prayed over Rosemary's belly, and I spoke to our daughter every night. I would speak the armor of God from Ephesians 6:10-18:

> "*Finally, be strong in the Lord and in his mighty power. Put on the full armor of God, so that you can take your stand against the devil's schemes. For our struggle is not against flesh and blood, but against the rulers, against the authorities, against the powers of this dark world and against the spiritual forces of evil in the heavenly realms. Therefore put on the full armor of God, so that when the day of evil comes, you may be able to stand your ground, and after you have done everything, to stand. Stand firm then, with the belt of truth buckled around your waist, with the breastplate of righteousness in place, and with your feet fitted with the readiness that comes from the gospel of peace. In addition to all this, take up the shield of faith, with which you can extinguish all the flaming arrows of the evil one. Take the helmet of salvation and the sword of the Spirit, which is the word of God. And pray in the Spirit on all occasions with all kinds of prayers and requests. With this in mind, be alert and always keep on praying for all the Lord's people.*

Every time I would say that scripture, I would kind of grin to myself because the first word of that scripture says, "finally... ." "Finally." That word just kept sticking in me every time I would read it, *"finally."* Finally, the Lord spoke to me one day as I was saying it. He said, "Yes, my son. *Finally.*" I said, "Yes, Lord, I get it." God said, "Finally, you're getting the hang of this. You're finally using your word, you're finally trusting in me to do the hard things."

But while giving birth, we realized April was in distress. The cord had wrapped around her neck and every time Rosemary had a contraction, the cord would choke April even more. I just remember God giving me the scripture about the full armor of God again.

> "Finally, be strong in the Lord and in his mighty power. Put on the full armor of God, so that you can take your stand against the devil's schemes. For our struggle is not against flesh and blood, but against the rulers, against the authorities, against the powers of this dark world and against the spiritual forces of evil in the heavenly realms. Therefore put on the full armor of God, so that when the day of evil comes, you may be able to stand your ground, and after you have done everything, to stand. Stand firm then, with the belt of truth buckled around your waist, with the breastplate of righteousness in place, and with your feet fitted with the readiness that comes from the gospel of peace. In addition to all this, take up the shield of faith, with which you can extinguish all the flaming arrows of the evil one. Take the helmet of salvation and the sword of the Spirit, which is the word of God. And pray in the Spirit on all occasions with all kinds of prayers and requests. With this in mind, be alert and always keep on praying for all the Lord's people.

I was learning that there was an enemy that wanted to take anything and everything from me. He wanted to have my family. He wanted to take my wife, my life. He didn't want me to know my true identity in God. God was right there and called me by my name over and over to remind me He was doing something beautiful in me. Something great was about to happen to me and it did! As Dr. Sandals continued to pray and speak to me, I just grinned and said,

"Yes, Lord, I get it, finally. I'm going to keep this full armor on."

The complications from the cord around her neck left us feeling helpless, but encouraged that with God's help, we would make it through all this. We knew that God would take care of April. He didn't bring April this far to not bring her to us healthy, whole, and vibrant. Finally, she was born. She was beautiful, too. Lots of hair, beautiful smile, a little, tiny nose, and red as a beet. She let out a big cry and just kept on crying. I couldn't wait to hold her. I couldn't wait to pray for her. I couldn't wait to be her father. I couldn't wait to love her. It actually hurt me when the nurse had to take her to the nursery in an incubator. I remember standing at the window looking helpless as they pricked my daughter's foot to take the blood for the very first time. I felt that pain so deep in my heart. I felt my daughter's pain and I thought, "God, is that how it feels when you see us hurting? God said, "Yes, Phillip, it does." I was able to feel her pain. I was swayed. I said, "God, don't ever take that away. I always want to be able to take care of her. I always want to be able to have a heart for my daughter."

After getting the perfect check-up, we took our daughter home. My mother-in-law came to help, and the baby was able to nurse with Rosemary right away. "God, you are so good to us." God said, "Yes, Phillip, I love you the same." I of course went back to work because that's what dad's do. They didn't give dad's time off back then, but man, I couldn't wait to get home at night to see my daughter. She was very talkative, outgoing, and active. She's bold like her mom. She was an old soul full of love and life. Very mature for her age. I remember when her birthday came, I went to the store to buy her a ball. I took it to the counter, then I went and put it back on the shelf. Then I took it back to the counter, then back to the shelf. I did this three or four times. I couldn't understand what was going on inside of me, but I was like, "Lord, I don't want to buy her love. I just want her to know that I love her genuinely. I don't want to buy her affection, but that I just want her to know that her father loves her."

Later that night, I had a dream of the devil throwing these material things of the world at me from atop this gigantic mountain in the distance. They just kept falling out of the sky onto this little boy (who was me). I said, "Lord, make it stop." God said, "Pick up that triangle stone over there and throw it at him." So, I did, and the devil ran away. Then suddenly, the material things stopped falling from the sky. I asked God for the interpretation of the dream. He said, "Whatever you need, I will provide," and that "love was pure and not to be bought, but to be freely given." See, my father had given me tons of material things when I was a child. I believe it was his way of trying to say I love you to me. He did not give me his time nor words of affirmation or physical touch. That's what I wanted more than anything. I wanted my father's acceptance and I wanted to know that he loved me. This is something that God was teaching me so that I could be different and break that cycle for my family. Our love was going to be the kind of love like God loved us. I wanted my children to know that they were the priority and that loving them was my honor and greatest joy. From that day forward, I showered my children with love. I told them that they were loved, and I tried to show them my love by being present in their lives. Rosemary and I chose to be God's kind of love to our children to the best of our ability. We wanted to raise them in the church, and we wanted them to know they were not just loved by us, but that they were loved by God that they were children of God. They were truly a gift from God.

    I remember April was two when she said, "I love you," back to me. I was on the top of the world after that. She said it all the time. This is what I am so proud of. She heard her dad say I love you to her and she was so ready to say it back. It just came natural for her. We have always been very close, April and I, and I love her with all my heart. Both her mother and I do. She was very close to us, and she worked with us in ministry and was a very good girl. In fact, she didn't even start dating until she was eighteen years old. I consider that quite an accomplishment nowadays.

    Now all these years later, my father has learned to say "I love you" to me and I can say it to him. In fact, we all say it to each other. It's a great legacy that we are building. My children can say it to me, I can say it to my father and to my children, and I know they say it to their children as well. I was twenty-four years old before I heard my father say those words and I was determined that would not be the case for my children. Rosemary and I showered our children with love. We told them that they were loved. We chose to put God first in our lives and to love our children the way God loved us. It was a choice. Rosemary and I didn't grow up that way, but we let God teach us how to do it for our children.

I love you. That's all God wants from you. All He's ever looking for are the people made in His image to be in a relationship with Him. We were created to love. We were created to need one another. He desires to need us and to have a relationship with us. That's all. God wants to be in a relationship with us where we say *I love you* not because we're forced, but because we truly understand His goodness. He wants us to be and stay in a right relationship with Him. That's always been His heart's desire. It's why we were created. It's why He keeps showing up and loving us the same.

God just wants us to be real with him so he can stay in relationship with us. It's us that try to be isolated or removed from Him. It's us who think that now that we're grown men and women, we no longer need Him. We think we're supposed to do everything all on our own, but that's not God's heart for us at all. He wants us to do it *with him.* It's His desire to help us, to teach us, to love on us, to encourage us, and most of all, to stand for us.

Jonathan

My son was a miracle baby also. He was born on June 14th, 1993. He was only one-and-a-half pounds, so he had to stay in the hospital till October 25th. As you know, prior to April, we had already lost four babies. We had April and now here we are again, pregnant. We were so excited to be having another child, a son. We felt thankful and very blessed by the Lord for giving us the desire of our hearts, but now here we are in NICU with a one-and-a-half-pound baby. He was so tiny, so delicate, so frail. As a father, I just felt so helpless. What can I even do for this poor child who has to be here in this incubator in this hospital? All I could do is to let him hear my voice, touch my hand, and pray for him. Being born early was the least of his concerns. The detaching of the placenta caused his birth to come so early that Rosemary had to be flown from one hospital to St Luke's Hospital in Houston. She was on complete bed rest. If she could hold on to the baby for forty-eight hours, the baby would have a 50/50 chance of living.

Rosemary held that baby for 7 *days*. 7 is the number of completion. Seven long days she held that baby inside her. She laid there perfectly still making sure that Jonathan had every opportunity at life. As she laid in that bed, she did not even get up to use the bathroom. She accepted her higher mission. She laid there in peace trusting in the Lord and resting in His perfect will, praying without ceasing, and trusting God to do the rest. During that time, the Lord spoke to me and said, "Focus on the baby's heart." I heard this a couple of times. "Focus on the baby's heart." When He tells me to do something, I hang on to every word. So, as I would pray, I would pray specifically for his heart. Then Rosemary called upset one day saying the doctor says this and that is wrong with Jonathan, but I just calmly said to her, "How is his heart?" She said, "His heart is fine." I said, "Well that's all I need to know. You have nothing to worry about, God is in control."

The day he was born, he was very tiny. We had 11 to 14 doctors all around Jonathan working on him. His whole foot was only 3/4 of an inch. As they got ready to bring him to her, I said, "Mama, he's going to be tiny, but don't focus on that, just focus on him. Be okay. See him as already being strong." I remember the first time sitting in the waiting room, the doctors would come out and tell various parents to get a hold of their priest. Rosemary and I just sat there not knowing if our turn would be next. There were so many parents in that waiting room that wanted nothing more than to take their child home and hearing the nurses come out and tell these parents one by one "It's time. Please go get your priest." "It's time" was horrifying to me. I said, "Lord, I don't want our name called." I did not know what was going to happen. All I wanted to know, Lord, is Jonathan next so I can prepare Rosemary. God said, "No, just focus on his heart."

The fear was so real. He stayed in that NICU for months. They were testing him all the time. They were telling us that he could have brain damage or this or that. I would call our church and ask for prayer. They were our family, and they would pray. They were ready if we ever needed blood or anything else. They constantly told us, "We are here for you. We are here for Jonathan." Others in the hospital, upon seeing the support we had, started coming to us and asking for prayer. There was this one boy named Michael who was in an incubator who we prayed for. I stretched out my hand

and I prayed with all the might I could muster. As soon as I did, the alarms went off. Later in the week, his mom said, "Thank you, he's now eating and gaining weight." We later went to his first birthday party. He was a happy healthy boy, just like Jonathan.

    We were weary during this time. We had a two-year-old at home and we were back and forth always dealing with doctors, tests, and procedures. They even talked about having to go into his heart and fix a vein. I said, "Oh no." But God. God warned us and God told us to pray for his heart. His heart is strong. Those the words I kept hearing in my head. Later that day, the doctor called back and said, "No, we decided not to go in. It will close itself." That was all God. Jonathan was a tiny baby, and yet, God loved him the same. He hadn't even had a chance at life and he didn't know how to worship the Lord. We played worship music all the time while Jonathan was growing, but he was not thriving in the incubator, so he was entered into the kangaroo program, which is the skin-to-skin program. The nurse had asked me if I wanted to start. I said, "No, his mama's waited long enough to hold him. Give him to her." Once we started that, he was doing much better. Finally, we were able to take him home. Jonathan's life touched so many doctors, nurses, and family members while we were there in that hospital. His little life was already a living testimony, and he hadn't even uttered a word yet.

    God always reminds me that these are His children; they are gifts to us. He will take care of them; He will protect them; our job is just love them. So, I just left them in God's hands because the Lord has the final say so. Our church celebrated with us when we were finally able to bring Jonathan to church. He flourished as a young boy. He served in the church. He is an incredible son and I am honored that God picked me to be his earthly father.

11

Becoming Parents

*"As a father has compassion on his children,
so the L*ORD *has compassion on those who fear him..."*
Psalm 103:13

We said we didn't want to be like our parents, so we made a vow, yet we were the same. Only God could make us different. While Rosemary was in the hospital, our daughter was three. Six ladies in the church took care of April during the day while I worked during Rosemary's hospitalization. The body of Christ really helped us. But with mama not there, I had to trust in Him and not my own ways. A couple of times I tried disciplining April and God said, "Phillip, she doesn't need discipline, she needs love." I even went to Pastor Gene and said, "I can't be an elder because I disciplined my daughter too harshly." Pastor Gene was so comforting. He just looked at me and said, "So, if you're coming to me and you already know what you did and that you've already corrected it, then that means the Holy Spirit already convicted you and therefore you don't need to condemn yourself. You need to continue to do the work that I have called you to do and that God has called you to do." See, we desire our Father God. We desire for him to fill a void. That's the void we are trying to fill with other things like relationships or drugs or alcohol, pornography, or being a workaholic. But you got to go to the root where Jesus is absent. Jesus will cut that root out. The lie that you believed, the traumas you endured, only Jesus can get that root out. God alone does the work in us in His timing.

Same thing with my son, Jonathan. If I was harsh with him like my father had been with me, then I had to repent to him even though I'm forgiven. It still hurts. I wish that I never made any mistakes. I wish that when I got saved, I was perfect, but that just isn't how it works. I pray that he's going to be okay. I thank God every day for His resurrection power. I thank God that my children will always know they are loved by their parents and by God. He loves them the same. I thank God for His grace and mercy which is new each and every day. The Holy Spirit is always quick to remind us we are still that little small boy or girl that God is perfecting and that we need to treat each other with love and kindness, with grace and mercy, and compassion. To love them the same as Christ loves us.

"Now that you have purified yourselves by obeying the truth so that you have sincere love for each other, love one another deeply, from the heart." 1 Peter 1:22

God doesn't expect you to spoil the children. He does want you to discipline them, but not in anger and frustration. He wants us to discipline them as a way of teaching them and growing them. Pray with them. Let them know right from wrong and His grace when they make mistakes. I remember one time when my daughter turned thirteen, she acted up at the grocery store thinking I would not discipline her in the store. But I said *I need to handle this in here right now.* Don't ever be afraid to discipline your children or bring correction, just don't discipline them from that place of anger. I looked at her and said, "Do you really want me to take care of this right now." She quickly changed her tune and got in her right mind because she knew I meant business.

God says in His word, he disciplines us because that is love.

"Because the Lord disciplines the one he loves,
and he chastens everyone he accepts as his son." Heb 12:6

A lot of times, we are rebellious not because we want to be rebellious, but because when we were disciplined or when we did make a mistake, we were disciplined out of anger which caused us to then want to lie or do things in secret because of that pain we suffered. Let that pain go. Give it to God and just know that when God disciplines, he does it in a tender and a loving way so that we can get better and be protected from the things of this world. He allows us to grow into a new mindset and have a right understanding of who He is to us and who we are to Him. He wants us to keep growing in and through Him.

You need to let your children go. Be willing to give them back to God, trusting that God will work everything out for His good, according to His perfect will. I remember right after my wife passed; my son still lived at home. I was going through her stuff and he told me he was moving out. One night, as he was reading about Peter stepping out of the boat, the Holy Spirit began showing him that it was time for him to step out of the boat as well. I was so happy he heard from God. So, I asked him if I could help him with his rent moving forward and he said, "no." I told him to remember, waves are coming. Storms came at Peter *after* Peter walked out of the boat. He fell when he took his eyes off Jesus, so remember, put your eyes on the Lord and remember the winds. Remember the waves. Remember that God will keep you as long as you keep your eyes on him. At that time, Jonathan was contending for his own marriage to be made whole and I was believing in agreement with him. Soon after he shared that with me, he went back to read his devotion. He had skipped one lesson the day before. And when he went back to it, it said, "Don't wait." He said, "Okay, Dad, I got to go." I said, "You know why you went back to the sixteenth of May? Because that was Mom and I's wedding anniversary. I believe Mom is showing you *don't wait*, tomorrow is not promised to anyone.

*"Do not boast about tomorrow,
for you do not know what a day may bring."* Pro 27:1

"So, son, don't put off what you need to do. Go and do it. Go and know that you are blessed. You are blessed by both your mom and I." So, you see, as a father myself, God has shown me what it means to show up as a father. To be a man. As my son obeyed and allowed God to heal his life, he and his wife were able to move in together and get an apartment. This is how God works. God promises to help the next generations after you. God showed me how I can show up for my son. I don't have to take away his ability to think or be a man. I just came alongside him and supported him. It's hard as a natural man of course. I don't want to see my children hurting, but I know that they are in the hands of the Lord. That is a promise God made me and Rosemary a long, long time ago.

A couple of months later, after leaving church, I was driving home. While I was on the road, I cried out to the Lord, "Lord, my son needs a home. I want him to have a better life. I don't want him to have struggles like I did." And as I was driving around, the Holy Spirit led me to turn here, turn there, and then I ended up in front of this home, and then a second home. The home that he showed me the second time ended up being the right home for them. I walked in and I had a peace. I didn't have a peace in the first house. I just felt like it wasn't quite right for them. The second home had trees in the back. My daughter-in-law said, "I always wanted an oak tree in my front yard, and Jonathan always wanted a pecan tree in the backyard. What's so funny is I always wanted my own fig tree. This house had all three! I took this as a sign. I immediately heard the Holy Spirit say, "This is the house," so I went into contract. I waited on God and when he said, "Now," I bought the home for them. I was so excited that with the Holy Spirit's help, I was able to be the tangible love of God to my son and his wife, God's daughter and God's son. When it was time to give them the keys to the home, the Holy Spirit had me pray this blessing over them:

"The Lord said this is your home. You will be able to lay your head on your own pillow. Have peace and rest by putting Me first in your life, marriage, and family. I will be here all the time. Through good times and difficult times. Remember that all decisions will come through y'all, Jonathan and Amalia. Listening to the Holy Spirit, He will give you the answers. You're going to hear counseling from other friends, believers, and even your dad and mom. Remember to always confirm it with the word of God. Jesus said it is written. Communication is a must! Praying together is a must! Going to church is a must! Giving God the tithe is a must! One more thing, never let your spouse turn his or her back and walk away from this home. By letting them go, you have opened the door for the enemy to move in! Keep that door closed in Jesus Christ's name. Amen"

It's important that I share some of this with you because I always thought my life might be different if my father on earth knew Christ like I did. But what I learned as a father is we all have to find Christ for ourselves. Just because I walk with God and live for Christ does not make me perfect or does not guarantee that my children and grandchildren won't go through hard times. What it does mean is this,

Jesus died for all of us. He wants all of us to walk with him. We all need to learn to trust in the Father, Son, and Holy Spirit. They are the key to living and prospering on this earth.

12

The Upper Room

"Then they returned to Jerusalem from the mount called Olivet, which is near Jerusalem, a Sabbath day's journey. And when they had entered, they went up into the upper room where they were staying: Peter, James, John, and Andrew; Phillip and Thomas; Bartholomew and Matthew; James the son of Alphaeus and Simon the Zealot; and Judas the son of James. These all continued with one accord in prayer and supplication, with the women and Mary the mother of Jesus, and with His brothers."
Acts 1:12-13

The upper room is a room in our home that I built later in Rosemary and I's marriage. It's where love resides. It's where Rosemary would go and soak in the presence of the Lord. It's where she would go and write the names of our family members on heart-shaped stones that she collected and kept in a box. She handwrote each person's name on a separate rock. It was her heart's desire to see every single one of our family members have a relationship with Jesus Christ and to be set free from their past. To know that they would come and be with her in heaven one day. She prayed prayers of war against the enemy and sowed seeds of love over the people in her family and her church family. Missionaries came and used that room. It was and is our prayer closet.

    I still go to that room. Whenever I want to feel close to her presence or I want to feel the presence of the Lord, I go to that room even though it's been three years ago since she graduated. Rest in peace, Rosemary. One day, while going through Rosemary's writings, I found this love letter. It was a love letter that Rosemary wrote to me while she was on a marriage encounter. She was talking about our marriage bed, and it was talking about the commitment that she wanted to make to our love and to honoring and respecting me. It was about running free and making moments together, being holy with one another, and having a new level of intimacy with one another. This healed my heart when she gave it to me. That just showed me that not only did she love me, but she loved me with the love of the Lord. She loved me. She wanted things to be even better. This was always my motivation too. It made me want to change. I wanted to be good. I wanted what God had for us, which was a higher level of intimacy that we don't even understand until we are right with God. Even now as I grieve, God is reminding me of His love. Rosemary's heart was to love me the same as God.

> *"The wife does not have authority over her own body but yields it to her husband. In the same way, the husband does not have authority over his own body but yields it to his wife."* 1 Cor 7:4

Her body was not hers and my body is not mine. She gave me her heart, not just her body, and I gave her mine. God says, "I'm giving all of me to all of you and so I expect the two of you to give all of yourselves to one another as well." It's part of being the three-stranded cord that cannot be easily broken.

> "Though one may be overpowered two can defend themselves. A cord of three strands is not quickly broken." Eccl 4:12

Our bodies are no longer our own, but belong to each other:

> "Marriage should be honored by all, and the marriage bed kept pure, for God will judge the adulterer and all the sexually immoral." Heb 13:4

God began to teach us that love did not look the way we thought it did. It did not feel the way we thought it did. He started teaching us 1 Corinthians 13 in a deep, more meaningful way:

> "Love is patient, love is kind. It does not envy, it does not boast, it is not proud. It does not dishonor others, it is not self-seeking, it is not easily angered, it keeps no record of wrongs. Love does not delight in evil but rejoices with the truth. It always protects, always trusts, always hopes, always perseveres. Love never fails. But where there are prophecies, they will cease; where there are tongues, they will be stilled; where there is knowledge, it will pass away. For we know in part, and we prophesy in part, but when completeness comes, what is in part

disappears. When I was a child, I talked like a child, I thought like a child, I reasoned like a child. When I became a man, I put the ways of childhood behind me. For now we see only a reflection as in a mirror; then we shall see face to face. Now I know in part; then I shall know fully, even as I am fully known. And now these three remain: faith, hope and love. But the greatest of these is love." 1 Cor 13

It's easy to say the words, but it's not so easy when you have to actually act them out or you have to actually put the other persons needs before your own. It's not easy when you have to actually be kind when someone's not being kind to you or patient when someone's not being patient with you. It's about not keeping track of the past or letting the devil remind you of other people's mistakes or flaws. It's about giving people a new grace and a new mercy each and every day. It's about growing up and no longer thinking selfishly like children. The greatest is love, faith, hope. Love others, think the best of them at all times. I recommend reading 1 Corinthians 13 aloud. Insert your name every place where the word "love" is. Use it as a checklist to make sure you are being like Christ to those around you.

"Because of the Lord's great love we are not consumed, for his compassions never fail. They are new every morning; great is your faithfulness." Lam 3:22-23

Vow of Praise

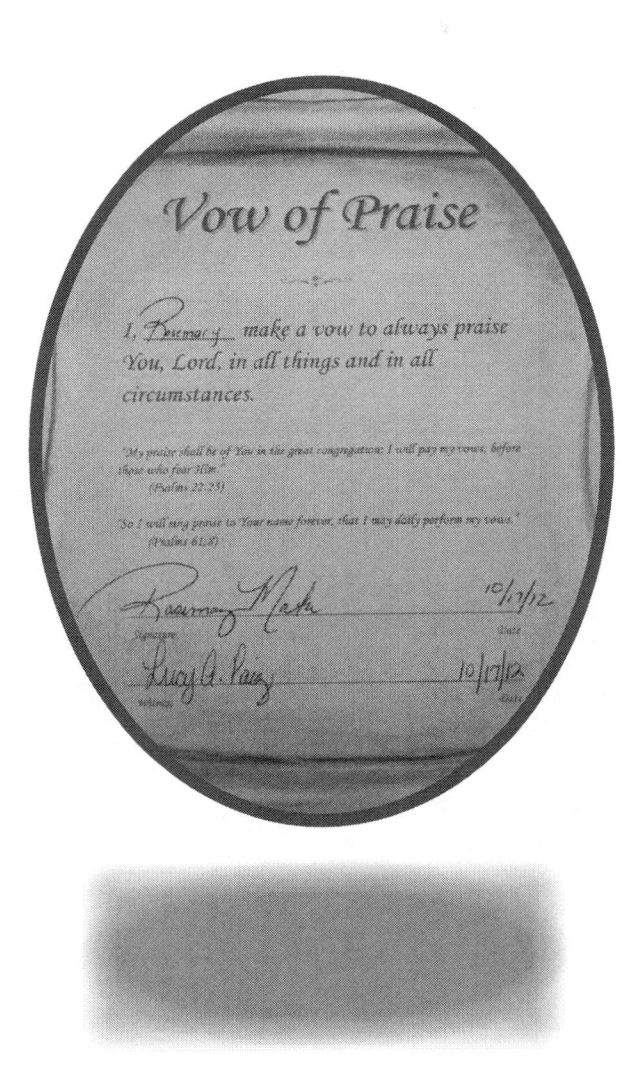

I, Rosemary, make a vow to always praise You, Lord, in all things and in all circumstances.

"My praise shall be of You in the great congregation; I will pay my vows before those who fear Him."
(Psalms 22:25)

"So I will sing praise to Your name forever, that I may daily perform my vows."
(Psalms 61:8)

_____ 10/17/12
Signature   Date

_____ 10/17/12
Witness   Date

13

God Is In The Details

"The Lord directs the steps of the godly. He delights in every detail of their lives. Though they stumble, they will never fall, for the Lord holds them by the hand."
Psalm 37: 23-24

Coincidence or God?

Back in the 60s, when I lived at my parents' house in the African area across the tracks on the northside of Rosenberg, my neighbor's dad worked for a crane company. We lived in a mostly Hispanic area, but I remember there was this older white man, an engineer, who would pick up my friend's dad, take him to work, and bring him home again. He had big, black framed glasses and was always smoking a cigarette. He had a very nice station wagon as well. I never forgot him because we honestly only saw black and Hispanics at that time on our side of town. Now let's fast forward fifteen years so you can see how God works. I go to the Church of Living Waters and I hear this great preacher. As he's preaching, I keep looking at him because he looks vaguely familiar. It turned out that the preacher was the same white man who used to come in my neighborhood and pick up my neighbor's father. It was Pastor Gene. This is the pastor who I learned from and sat under for the remainder of my walk until he went home to be with the Lord. Look at how this man changed in fifteen years' time. God said to me, "I have everything under control."

God is into the littlest of details. I've been at the same church from age 24 to age 60, 36 years, and I'm still here. In fact, I'm currently serving in the children's ministry. (Rosemary and I did leave for a brief moment to do something for God, but then we came right back). Church is not just a building; church is a family. Church is a body of believers. Each of us has a role to play.

> "So Christ himself gave the apostles, the prophets, the evangelists, the pastors and teachers, to equip his people for works of service, so that the body of Christ may be built up until we all reach unity in the faith and in the knowledge of the Son of God and become mature, attaining to the whole measure of the fullness of Christ. Then we will no longer be infants, tossed back and forth by the waves, and blown here and there by every wind of teaching and by the cunning and craftiness of people in their deceitful scheming. Instead, speaking the truth in love, we will grow to become in every respect the mature body of him who is the head, that is, Christ. From him the whole body, joined and held together by every supporting ligament, grows and builds itself up in love, as each part does its work." Eph 4:11-16

Church is a family to me just like your own family. You may fuss, you may fight, but you always stay, and you always work things out. We are all needed in the body. One thing that all believers must understand is that we are all going to go through seasons of change. It's a part of life. But no matter what we go through, we have to keep standing. You may get knocked down seven times, but you must get up eight times. We all will go through trials and tribulations, that is a guarantee. How we respond to those trials and tribulations is what separates us from the rest of the world. In the early years of my Christianity, late 80s-early 90s, I experienced a church split. Yes, the church split. Most of my brothers and sisters in the Lord who I was growing with and having Bible studies with decided to leave one by one. As they were leaving, I asked God, "Lord, am I to leave, too?" God said, "No, stay still. Do not be moved by what you see or what you hear. Stand firm. Stand on the word only. Be moved by me." I continued and continue to be faithful to the Church of Living Waters.

Acts of Disobedience

The Holy Spirit reminded me of a time around 2007-2008 when Rosemary and I left the church for a couple of years. We felt we were being led by The Holy Spirit. So, to get confirmation, we went to the pastor and his wife, Betty Jo. She said, "Where are you going? I said, "We're not sure, but this is a good thing. We won't be taking any sheep with us. We are just going to be obedient to God." So, we jumped into another church instead of waiting on what the Lord had for us. I should've gone back to the Lord to make sure that this is what He wanted us to do, but I didn't. I was passive and listened to my wife and daughter. And because of my passivity, we went through a lot. But thankfully, God was merciful in all of it. It was always my heart to just make Rosemary happy and so I was afraid to say no. Truth be told, I was afraid she would leave me if I didn't agree to their wants in this church. God saw my heart and had grace for us in that season.

There was nothing wrong with the other church; it just was not where God wanted us to be. We jumped into ministry there. Rosemary helped in children's church. But when it was time to go, I knew. During the service one Sunday, I just got up and left. Rosemary, who was teaching another class, called me on my phone and said, "Where are you? Come and get me. It's time for me to leave." We repented to God and waited for the Holy Spirit to lead us to a place called The Lord's Kitchen that served and fed homeless people and others in need. We continued to serve there while we waited patiently on the Lord to tell us where he wanted us to go. And even though I had a word from the Lord, I didn't share it with Rosemary. I kept it to myself. It was a word for a group of people. I wasn't sure who it was for, but I knew we needed to wait until we were under a church to give it. So, I waited with that word inside me.

> *"Now there was a Pharisee, a man named Nicodemus who was a member of the Jewish ruling council. He came to Jesus at night and said, "Rabbi, we know that you are a teacher who has come from God. For*

no one could perform the signs you are doing if God were not with him." Jesus replied, "Very truly I tell you, no one can see the kingdom of God unless they are born again." "How can someone be born when they are old?" Nicodemus asked. "Surely they cannot enter a second time into their mother's womb to be born!" Jesus answered, "Very truly I tell you, no one can enter the kingdom of God unless they are born of water and the Spirit. Flesh gives birth to flesh, but the Spirit gives birth to spirit. You should not be surprised at my saying, 'You must be born again.' The wind blows wherever it pleases. You hear its sound, but you cannot tell where it comes from or where it is going. So it is with everyone born of the Spirit." "How can this be?" Nicodemus asked. "You are Israel's teacher," said Jesus, "and do you not understand these things? Very truly I tell you, we speak of what we know, and we testify to what we have seen, but still you people do not accept our testimony. I have spoken to you of earthly things and you do not believe; how then will you believe if I speak of heavenly things? No one has ever gone into heaven except the one who came from heaven—the Son of Man. Just as Moses lifted up the snake in the wilderness, so the Son of Man must be lifted up, that everyone who believes may have eternal life in him." For God so loved the world that he gave his one and only Son, that whoever believes in him shall not perish but have eternal life. For God did not send his Son into the world to condemn the world, but to save the world through him. Whoever believes in him is not condemned, but whoever does not believe stands condemned already because they have not believed in the name of God's one and only Son. This is the verdict: Light has come into the world, but people loved darkness instead of light because their deeds were evil. Everyone who does evil hates the light, and will not come into the light for fear that their deeds will be exposed. But whoever lives by the truth comes into the light, so that it may be seen plainly that what they have done has been done in the sight of God." John 3:1-21

One day, when we were at The Lord's Kitchen, we saw Pastor Gene's wife, Betty Jo. She came over to Rosemary and said, "I'm going to pray a selfish prayer. I pray you and Phillip will come back to Living Waters." This was Thanksgiving week. We just laughed and gave her a hug knowing that her heart was in the right place. Gene and Betty Jo were still family to us. Soon, December rolled around. Christmas was right around the corner. We were preparing for the holidays and praying and asking God where do we need to be. Then we got a call from the elders of the Church of Living Water that changed everything. On December 26th, we were told by the elders that Pastor Betty Jo and her daughter were hurt. The elders from the church called to give us this news and told us that we were needed at the hospital. I flew into action. I told them to come and pick me up. Once they got to me, they told me that *someone* had passed away at a hospital and that we needed to go see Pastor Gene who was at a different hospital separate from his family. When I got to Pastor Gene's hospital room, I just saw him in the state he was in. It was not good. In that moment, I knew this was my church family for life. Rosemary and I decided that we would get back to our home church.

Soon after this, we became a deacon, an elder, and later a minister. But in that moment, I was just a brother in the Lord. Seeing our spiritual family in need and in hurt, all we wanted to do was offer our support in any way possible. They had given so much to us over the years as a couple and as a family that all we wanted to do was give back to them in this moment. They had loved us, fed us, and discipled us.

When we got to the room and saw the pastor covered in blood, they were going to discharge him in those clothes. I just took off my shirt and gave it to my brother, my pastor, my spiritual father, to the one who married us and loved us for all these years. Tears rolled down my face as he was in need. It was my honor to serve him in that moment and from then till today.

Rosemary and I continued to serve in that church. I'm still there helping to serve the mens ministry. Rosemary's there in spirit. I'll go wherever and do whatever Pastor Darren, Pastor Gene's son, needs me to do. I can't give more details than that about that night or about the horrific thing that our church went through due to the legalities of the prior events. However, the first words that came out Pastor Gene's mouth as we saw him was, "I forgive James." It was important for me to share my heart about how God showed up for Rosemary and I and showed us His mercy and grace during that trying time. God knows who needs you. God knows where he needs you to be. You're part of a body. It's not about how you feel; it's about what God needs; it's about you being a part of a working body. I share that story to also show you that even pastors go through hard things. Members of your church go through hard things. But it's okay, we're a family. We stick together, no matter what!

Not only did we serve our church and our local community, we also traveled to other places and lands such as Italy, Turkey, Venezuela, and Mexico. Anywhere that God needed us to serve, we went and served. If any pastors from those countries needed a place to stay, we would house them when they came to Rosenberg. It was just about serving God and being a part of the work that God needed us to do.

Currently, I am teaching in the children's church at Church of Living Water and loving every minute of it. I also help with the prison ministry and in our mens home called The Sheepfold. But most importantly I just serve my father. I want to not only be a leader that can lead others to the Lord, I also want to be like my God who has been my father. He's our Father who has adopted us, therefore, just as he has adopted us, we are to adopt one another into the kingdom. He is not only just a father, He is a father that cares, a father that listens, and a father that truly loves us.

> "I tell you, my friends, do not be afraid of those who kill the body and after that can do no more. But I will show you whom you should fear: Fear him who, after your body has been killed, has authority to throw you into hell. Yes, I tell you, fear him. Are not five sparrows sold for two pennies? Yet not one of them is forgotten by God. Indeed, the very hairs of your head are all numbered. Don't be afraid; you are worth more than many sparrows." Luke 12:4-7

> "Because you are his sons, God sent the Spirit of his Son into our hearts, the Spirit who calls out, " Abba, Father." Gal 4:6

Tithing

One of the greatest teachings I learned from Pastor Gene at Church of Living Waters was tithing. One Sunday, I had a brother in the church ask me if I was tithing. I said, "No." I was in bed at this time. Rosemary had been handling the bills and we were starting to get behind on them. After Rosemary and I separated, I had to handle the bills. I was sitting at the kitchen table with a stack of bills staring back at me. I was just lost. How am I going to pay all of these bills? At that moment, God said to me, "My tithe." "How am I supposed to do that, God? I am barely above water. After God asked twice, I let out a sigh and then I pulled out my checkbook and wrote the tithe check. Then God said, "Now, pay the bills." "How?" "Pay the bills." I said, "Okay, Lord," and started writing out all the bills. Not only did I pay every bill, I had $120 left over. I just wept. "God, you are who you say you are, and I trust you. I trust you with all the details of my life and my family's life." God put Rosemary and I back together. We remarried on May 16, 1987

In 2018, I retired. At that time, I was making a lot less money. One day, my wife said, "Hey, are you aware that every time you give, God gives us back more? I said, "Huh? What are you talking about, Rosemary?" "Every time you give, God gives us back more." God used to do this very amazing thing with us. He would speak to us individually about the amount of tithe/love offering he wanted us to give, then we would confer with each other, and it would be the same amount *every time*. One time, God said, "Give

$500," to me for a guest speaker who's doing God's ministry. I was like, "Wow, that's kind of high, Lord." So, I asked Rosemary, "Hey, how much did the Lord tell you to give." She turned to me and said, "God said give a thousand." I just laughed, "Okay Lord, I guess I should've paid the $500." God was stretching us and testing our faith. He was teaching us to trust him, believe in Him, and believe in His word. It is the truth.

One of my prayers I used to say to God during this time was, "Lord, I want to be able to give like I did when I worked all that overtime." God said, "You are." I didn't realize I had been. I was not giving according to what was coming in, I was giving according to what God asked me to. *And He's replacing it!* Was I buying the pastor's suit? No, I was sewing into the kingdom! I hear this all the time, *"It's not my responsibility to take care of the building. It's not my responsibility to pay the pastor's bills."* No, it's not. That's God's responsibility. God's asking us to be faithful with the part that belongs to Him. We are to build a storehouse and we are to be obedient with God's ten percent. That's God's money. He's the one who stretches us. He's the one who makes that ten percent stretch to meet the people's needs.

> *"Will a mere mortal rob God? Yet you rob me.*
> *"But you ask, 'How are we robbing you?' "In tithes and offerings. You are under a curse—your whole nation—because you are robbing me. Bring the whole tithe into the storehouse, that there may be food in my house. Test me in this," says the Lord Almighty, "and see if I will not throw open the floodgates of heaven and pour out so much blessing that there will not be room enough to store it."*
> *Mal 3: 8-10*

This includes spiritual food and the church's ability to care for the orphans and widows. God tests, the devil tempts.

> "Religion that God our Father accepts as pure and faultless is this: to look after orphans and widows in their distress and to keep oneself from being polluted by the world." James 1:27

Wonderful Teacher

God is a wonderful teacher. Even though I went through both good and bad things growing up and didn't know how to be a husband, a man, or a father, God taught me everything I needed to know, and he is still teaching me. It doesn't matter if you have a relationship with your earthly father or not, if you cry out to Abba Father and say, "God, teach me," and then you really open up your heart and humble yourself, God will teach you. He will take it one day at a time with you and he will show you exactly what you need to do. Will you be perfect? No. It's not about perfection; it's about being humble.

I never knew God was listening to me all those times I cried out at night, but once I got saved and surrendered, I found out He listened to every word that I said. Before Christ, I would say, "God, are you real? If you're real, teach me how to walk on this earth. Your word says, "You will know the truth and the truth will always set you free." I wanted to be free. I needed to be free. I needed God. Oh God, how I want that freedom. I want to be free. Free from rejection. Free from loneliness. Free from hurt. Free from abandonment. Free from the lies in my thoughts that nobody cares, nobody loves me, nobody wants me.

I encourage you today if you have felt those things, don't be ashamed. Just know God hears you and God says, "Yes! Yes, you are loved. Yes, someone does care. Yes, somebody does love you. I am right here to walk by your side through all of it. Just come and seek me."

> *"In the same way, I tell you, there is rejoicing in the presence of the angels of God over one sinner who repents."*
> Luke 15:10

Once you taste and see what the Lord has for you, it will excite you. As a baby Christian, you're going to be all zealous for the Lord. Longevity, patience, and grace is what you need. For most people that are baby Christians, you think you're on top of the world. You think you're unstoppable. I felt loved and protected. I know there was nothing else the enemy could do to me, but it didn't stop the enemy from trying. Here I am all these years later and I'm letting you know, Satan is always going to test you. Satan is always looking for an opportunity to kill your purpose, steal your identity, and destroy your destiny. It's your responsibility to stay close by God's side. You're always going to be learning; you're always going to be growing; and you're always going to need God right by your side.

PS: I Love You

"... that you may be children of your Father in heaven. He causes his sun to rise on the evil and the good, and sends rain on the righteous and the unrighteous." Matthew 5:45

Thirty-five years ago, God said, "Phillip, something beautiful is going to happen in your life and you're going to change for the best." I had no idea what He meant. But having that promise is what I hold on to every single day. Whether I have a good day or a bad day, I hold on to that because I know every day is a new day in God. I remind God what He told me. Through all of my ups and downs, one thing remained constant... He loves me the same.

14

Rosemary's Funeral

Oscar, Pastor Darren, April, and I stood with the coffin open. As we prepared for the service, The Holy Spirit began to speak to me. He said, "Anoint Rosemary with some oil." So, I put some on her forehead, face, and neck. Then I looked at Pastor Darren and said, "Would it be okay if I kiss her one last time?" He shook his head and said, "Of course." The coffin was pink and there were sprays of flowers draped over it. Roses in every color, red and white flower arrangements, and other flower arrangements that people had given to her for her going home ceremony. At the pulpit are Pastor Lauren and Pastor Darren. To the right in all black is worshiper Carl Vincent with one guitar player behind him in a black outfit and black hat. To the left was Phillip Wu. All the way to the left was Pastor Rudy Cantu. Sitting in chairs are Pastor Roger Paiz and Pastor Rufus

Guebara and Pastor Rob Wisdom. Behind them were deep blue curtains with lights individually cascading down like stars. My wife, my one true love, was gone. And now we are getting ready to celebrate her graduation to heaven, but my heart is hurting. All I want is for her to be here sitting next to me. Our church, this is where we served God for more than 30+ years. This is our family, our friends, our fellow pastors, and those that we have been doing life with all these years. Everyone is here but her. Pastor Ismo Morin doesn't open with a prayer, instead he reads Psalm 136:

> *"Give thanks to the Lord, for he is good.*
> *His love endures forever.*
> *Give thanks to the God of gods.*
> *His love endures forever.*
> *Give thanks to the Lord of lords:*
> *His love endures forever.*
> *to him who alone does great wonders,*
> *His love endures forever.*
> *who by his understanding made the heavens,*
> *His love endures forever.*
> *who spread out the earth upon the waters,*
> *His love endures forever.*
> *who made the great lights—*
> *His love endures forever.*
> *the sun to govern the day,*
> *His love endures forever.*
> *the moon and stars to govern the night;*
> *His love endures forever.*
> *to him who struck down the firstborn of Egypt*
> *His love endures forever.*
> *and brought Israel out from among them*
> *His love endures forever.*
> *with a mighty hand and outstretched arm;*
> *His love endures forever.*

PS: I Love You

> to him who divided the Red Sea[a] asunder
> His love endures forever.
> and brought Israel through the midst of it,
> His love endures forever.
> but swept Pharaoh and his army into the Red Sea;
> His love endures forever.
> to him who led his people through the wilderness;
> His love endures forever.
> to him who struck down great kings,
> His love endures forever.
> and killed mighty kings—
> His love endures forever.
> Sihon king of the Amorites
> His love endures forever.
> and Og king of Bashan—
> His love endures forever.
> and gave their land as an inheritance,
> His love endures forever.
> an inheritance to his servant Israel.
> His love endures forever.
> He remembered us in our low estate
> His love endures forever.
> and freed us from our enemies.
> His love endures forever.
> He gives food to every creature.
> His love endures forever.
> Give thanks to the God of heaven.
> His love endures forever."

Rosemary understood God's mercy. She knew what it was to be without Him. She experienced His mercy and He drove her near to the Sun to celebrate her life today. "Well done my good and faithful daughter." Pastor Ruby came up next. As he stated her name, "Rosemary," I saw the word 'rose'. When I heard Pastor Rudy say this, I thought of the word that the Lord gave me about the rose and how it was beautiful inside and out. I even wrote it on a paper. Pastor

Rudy went on to say she was a beautiful lady inside and out. She did ministry with me and my wife for many years. I would ask Rosemary if she wanted to speak and she would always say, "No, thank you," but I would hand her the mic anyway. I just had to lean in push her button because the beauty of the Lord was all around her.

    Pastor Darren was standing up there trying to be a pillar of strength, yet he was moved. Tears streamed down his face. He moved in love and compassion, swaying in the presence of the Lord as we continued the service. He was more than just compassionate; Pastor Darren honored my wife. Soon, the worship began. Rosemary loved to worship so we honored her life in a song and a praise unto the Lord. First, we sang "Taste and see that the Lord is good." And then we sang "Lord, I am amazed by you." People stood and joined in song raising their hands to the Lord. Even though I was in the front, I knew that family members and friends and people from all over joined with me in celebrating my Rosemary's life. I was witnessing more than just the woman that I loved, but the minister that she was as well. This was our legacy. This is what we worked for. This is what we had done with our lives together after God had spared ours and gave us a second chance.

    All the pastors were on stage standing and worshiping through their tears, raising their hands in full surrender to the Lord God Almighty. As the songs played, our daughter, April, was standing singing. Rosemary's siblings were there. Her parents were there. She would have been so happy to know that they all came. Pastor Roger Paiz stood and read Psalm 23:

> "The Lord is my shepherd, I lack nothing.
> He makes me lie down in green pastures,
> he leads me beside quiet waters,
> he refreshes my soul.
> He guides me along the right paths
> for his name's sake.
> Even though I walk
> through the darkest valley,
> I will fear no evil,
> for you are with me;
> your rod and your staff,
> they comfort me.
> You prepare a table before me
> in the presence of my enemies.
> You anoint my head with oil;
> my cup overflows.
> Surely your goodness and love will follow me
> all the days of my life, and I will dwell in the house of
> the Lord forever."

Next was Audie Wright. My family and his went camping every year for over twenty years. He said, "Rosemary came to church with purpose. She raised her children with that purpose. She truly spoke to others in love. When she spoke truth, it was in love. She was a purposeful woman who set her eyes like flint. He read John 14:2-3:

> "My Father's house has many rooms; if that were not so, would I have told you that I am going there to prepare a place for you? And if I go and prepare a place for you, I will come back and take you to be with me that you also may be where I am."

Surely goodness and mercy shall follow you all the days....

"Good morning, Rosemary," said Rosemary's most precious and dear friend, Paz. As far as I know, she was more than just her dear friend, she was a confident for over 20 years. "Everything is going to be okay," Rosemary would say. "She was called, she was saved, and she was anointed," she said in her whisper of a voice. At the end, she spoke a Psalm and said, "Surely goodness and mercy shall follow you. Your family will see you well, I told her." "A woman of her word, she fought for her family. In the 80s, we met at this particular church, and we served together for over fifteen years. She heard from the Lord very clearly. She got me a job at Walmart. Walmart was her chapel. She prayed with others there. She witnessed to others. If she didn't agree, she would say, "I will have to go talk to Jesus about this." Jonathan, you need to know you were a miracle child. April, she's all her daddy, but she looks like her mom. She always had her tablet and her pen. Rosemary always wanted to hear from the Lord and was always prepared to do so. I'm a survivor of cancer twice, but Rosemary was always there praying for me. Always there for me. She's a woman with convictions. A woman who would not waiver. She sewed and served God with a purpose, on purpose. I asked God, "Why her?" He answered me Acts 20:24, she finished her race:

> *"However, I consider my life worth nothing to me; my only aim is to finish the race and complete the task the Lord Jesus has given me—the task of testifying to the good news of God's grace."*

She finished her test. She ran her race, and she did not waste her time. She was about her father's business. Then she read a text from Daniel Gabbar who googled what 'rose' meant. "Rosemary, if you were to Google it, it comes up *love*. A rose is love: love for her family, love for her God, love for her savior." As the service continued, you could feel the presence of God and the Holy Spirit. Next came Pastor Rob Wisdom came to the pulpit to speak. The Holy Spirit touched me as Rob spoke, "Lord, you are near to the broken-hearted and those who mourn. You are the hope to the hopeless, Father."

> *"The Lord is close to the brokenhearted*
> *and saves those who are crushed in spirit.*
> *The righteous person may have many troubles,*
> *but the Lord delivers him from them all;*
> *he protects all his bones,*
> *not one of them will be broken."* Psalm 34:18-20

Pastor Rob continued, "God, you are the answer. We honor her life. We give thanks for you sharing her with us and we give her back to you because she belongs to you."

> *"Some of those present were saying indignantly to one another, "Why this waste of perfume?"* Mark 14:4

"We were so honored to pray with you, Phillip and Rosemary, before you departed for your trip to Italy. Now Rosemary has departed, and you all have been a part of preparing her for this great departure. Remember, it's not how we see her, but how God sees her. She is His daughter and His completed work. She is his queen, his bride. Just like the woman who prepared Jesus for his burial because he had taken all her shame, she never saw it as a waste. Her life was a living sacrifice for her King Jesus. Her ministry was to those in Walmart, to those in third world countries. Every prayer was on purpose none of it was a waste."

As Pastor Rob spoke, the Lord reminded me of Rosemary's prayer room and her box. (*Rosemary had an alabaster box that she treasured. It was a box full of heart-shaped rocks she collected that were different sizes. She had each one of her family members names written on those rocks. Many were saved and will be. She prayed without ceasing and she knows her Father will answer her.*) Rosemary understood how precious salvation was and it was worth it to her to intercede for all of her family, her friends, and even those she didn't yet know. No one stayed a stranger long. Once Rosemary knew you, she knew her mission was to make sure that you knew Jesus.

Now I know why I anointed her for burial. It was to honor her and to honor the race that she won. It was also to anoint her for being the wife, the mother, the sister, the daughter, and the servant that Christ had asked her to be. Since she did so willingly, God will continue to use

Rosemary even after her death. Just as God did for Abel, all those prayers, all those tears will never go in vain. God heard every one of them, collected every one of them, and He will make sure that her prayers are answered.

Pastor Rob's wife sang a song she wrote. The lyrics went like this, *"Don't be afraid/just believe what I say/I'm the way, the truth, and the life always/don't be afraid."* Then she sang it again in Spanish. They went on to speak about the anointing for burial. The anointing of the Holy Spirit was there. But when he did an altar call, no one stood up at first. It became silent in there. I just closed my eyes and I just prayed in the spirit knowing that the Holy Spirit was doing something glorious in honor of Rosemary on this day. And then one by one, first her sister-in-law, then her son's wife, her daughter-in-law, stood. Then both her mother and her father stood, then her daughter, April, and her husband, then our son, Jonathan, then Rosemary's sister, then many others began to stand in unison. They all said the sinner's prayer. I don't know what God was doing; I just know that God was touching lives and hearts.

I know this pleased my beautiful Rosemary. And a side note for those who are reading this and are conflicted on whether you should give your life to the Lord. I'm here to tell you, it does not matter what people think of you or I, it matters what God thinks of you. It matters that Jesus is in you and that you are not ashamed of Jesus Christ. If you don't yet know Christ, the sinner's prayer is in the back of this book. I encourage you to find it and say it today.

After a moment of silence, they sang the song, "I Can Only Imagine" as a slideshow of the family played. It was a slideshow of Rosemary with her friends, her family, and her loved ones. It was a slideshow of the inheritance she left behind. At the end of the tribute, a picture of a single sunflower behind a bright blue sky stayed on the screen. Then my daughter got up to speak and the Holy Spirit told me, "Go stand beside her." I stood and joined her on stage. Then my sweet daughter, April, closed the graduation ceremony by saying, "It's going to be okay. The definition of the word okay was humble. She was a warrior dancing in the throne room. Where do we go from here? I hear my mom saying, "Keep going. Don't give up." She won her race. You are a child of God, and you have a race to win as well, so keep going. Don't give up."

> "Brothers and sisters, I do not consider myself yet to have taken hold of it. But one thing I do: Forgetting what is behind and straining toward what is ahead, I press on toward the goal to win the prize for which God has called me heavenward in Christ Jesus." Phil 3:13-14

Let go of the past and reaching for the things of tomorrow

15

The Resurrection Power

"Jesus said to her, "I am the resurrection and the life. He who believes in Me, though he may die, he shall live." John 11:25

After Rosemary passed away, I was driving out to the prison with Pastor Rudy. We were going to go see the prisoners. I was the passenger. I remember looking out the window and I saw a dead body on the side of the road. We turned around and headed back. Flies were already on the man. Pastor Rudy said, "This boy overdosed. I'm going to go call the police." I took a picture of the guy. He was definitely dead. As we stood by him waiting for the police, all of a sudden, the boy sat up! I said to the boy, "You were dead. You need to praise God that you're alive again." Right about then, the emergency crew got there and took over. Pastor Rudy and I hopped back in the car and proceeded to head to the prison. He looked at me and said, "What just happened? What's God showing us?" God said, "I could have done this for Rosemary." "I remember, Lord. I have no doubt that you can and that you could. And then He kept saying the scripture to me, "The wages of sin is death but the gift of God is eternal life."

"For the wages of sin is death, but the gift of God is eternal life in Christ Jesus our Lord." Rom 6:23

"Yes, Lord, we believed for her healing. We believed for healing in her body." I heard this more than three times from the Lord. The Lord said to me, *"The wages of sin is death, but the gift of God is eternal life."* At this point, Rosemary had been diagnosed with cancer. She actually was diagnosed on November 5, 2018, and passed away a month later on December 7, 2018.

Prior to her being diagnosed, I felt death come upon me in our home. I told Rosemary, "I think I'm dying. Please take care of the children and yourself." She said, "Of course, Phillip, I will." It was an eerie feeling that I had, and I couldn't shake it. I cried out to God, "Lord, I'm not ready to go home. I still feel I have a lot to do. Your word said we can have heaven here on earth and I want it here on earth with Rosemary." Of course, I want heaven and I know that I'm going to heaven, but I want to have heaven here, too. I want more time with Rosemary and the kids. A few days later, Rosemary was diagnosed. A month later, she passed. My heart hurt. All I wanted was for us to have more time.

"Tomorrow is not promised to us." We must live in the moment and be grateful for what and who God has given to us. God is in control and the sooner you surrender your will for what He has for you, the sooner you will know God loves you the same.

The Bible is the inspired word of God…

The word of God is alive. It is God speaking directly to you and to I. It's meant to heal you, teach you, and grow you into your purpose and destiny.

> *"Through the LORD's mercies we are not consumed,*
> *Because His compassions fail not.*
> *They are new every morning;*
> *Great is Your faithfulness." Lamentations 3:22-23*

> *"All Scripture is breathed out by God and profitable for teaching, for reproof, for correction, and for training in righteousness." 2 Timothy 3:16*

We are the church. We are all disciples. We are all ordained by God. We are all needed in order to build His kingdom and to set the captives free.

Phillip & Rosemary Mata

"For just as the body is one and has many members, and all the members of the body, though many, are one body, so it is with Christ. For in one Spirit we were all baptized into one body—Jews or Greeks, slaves or free—and all were made to drink of one Spirit.

For the body does not consist of one member but of many. If the foot should say, "Because I am not a hand, I do not belong to the body," that would not make it any less a part of the body. ¹⁶ And if the ear should say, "Because I am not an eye, I do not belong to the body," that would not make it any less a part of the body. If the whole body were an eye, where would be the sense of hearing? If the whole body were an ear, where would be the sense of smell? But as it is, God arranged the members in the body, each one of them, as he chose. If all were a single member, where would the body be? As it is, there are many parts, yet one body.

The eye cannot say to the hand, "I have no need of you," nor again the head to the feet, "I have no need of you." On the contrary, the parts of the body that seem to be weaker are indispensable, and on those parts of the body that we think less honorable we bestow the greater honor, and our unpresentable parts are treated with greater modesty, which our more presentable parts do not require. But God has so composed the body, giving greater honor to the part that lacked it, that there may be no division in the body, but that the members may have the same care for one another. If one member suffers, all suffer together; if one member is honored, all rejoice together.

Now you are the body of Christ and individually members of it." 1 Cor 12:12-27

Wherever you work, wherever you shop, wherever you go, you can be the tangible love of God. You can share the love of God. You just have to be willing and obedient. Yes, even in Walmart. Walmart was Rosemary's mission field in her latter days.

If someone was ill, she took them into the back office, laid hands on them, and cast that devil right out of them. Another time, she led an 18-year-old employee to Jesus who then enlisted in the military, became a chaplain, and started four churches in Guam. Be a disciple and make a disciple, that's the work of Jesus Christ.

> *"And he went up on the mountain and called to him those whom he desired, and they came to him. And he appointed twelve (whom he also named apostles) so that they might be with him and he might send them out to preach and have authority to cast out demons."*
> Mk3:13-15 ESV

> *"Now when Jesus had entered Capernaum, a centurion came to Him, pleading with Him, saying, "Lord, my servant is lying at home paralyzed, dreadfully tormented." And Jesus said to him, "I will come and heal him." The centurion answered and said, "Lord, I am not worthy that You should come under my roof. But only speak a word, and my servant will be healed. For I also am a man under authority, having soldiers under me. And I say to this one, 'Go,' and he goes; and to another, 'Come,' and he comes; and to my servant, 'Do this,' and he does it." When Jesus heard it, He marveled, and said to those who followed, "Assuredly, I say to you, I have not found such great faith, not even in Israel! And I say to you that many will come from east and west, and sit down with Abraham, Isaac, and Jacob in the kingdom of heaven. But the sons of the kingdom will be cast out into outer darkness. There will be weeping and gnashing of teeth." Then Jesus said to the centurion, "Go your way; and as you have believed, so let it be done for you." And his servant was healed that same hour."* Mt 8:5-13

We don't have to see the final product to know that God's word never returns void. We are to be a people of faith. That's God's promise that when we serve Him and do his work, we will reap a harvest of souls.

"And let us not grow weary while doing good, for in due season we shall reap if we do not lose heart." Gal 6:9

Like for my Aunt Lorene, she wanted her sister to be saved, but instead, she led me to Christ, and then later, God used to me to lead my mom to Christ. The goodness of God. It's His way and His timing. Period.

PS: I Love You

Epilogue

Now, three years later, I am still in tears as I watch this video of Rosemary's funeral. She led such a great life and God always loved her. As a believer or even an unbeliever, it doesn't change based on what you do or what you don't do. Our love changes, His doesn't. His Love is unconditional. It remains the same.

> "If I speak in the tongues of men or of angels, but do not have love, I am only a resounding gong or a clanging cymbal. If I have the gift of prophecy and can fathom all mysteries and all knowledge, and if I have a faith that can move mountains, but do not have love, I am nothing. If I give all I possess to the poor and give over my body to hardship that I may boast, but do not have love, I gain nothing. Love is patient, love is kind. It does not envy, it does not boast, it is not proud. It does not dishonor others, it is not self-seeking, it is not easily angered, it keeps no record of wrongs. Love does not delight in evil but rejoices with the truth. It always protects, always trusts, always hopes, always perseveres. Love never fails. But where there are prophecies, they will cease; where there are tongues, they will be stilled; where there is knowledge, it will pass away. For we know in part and we prophesy in

> *part, but when completeness comes, what is in part disappears. When I was a child, I talked like a child, I thought like a child, I reasoned like a child. When I became a man, I put the ways of childhood behind me. For now we see only a reflection as in a mirror; then we shall see face to face. Now I know in part; then I shall know fully, even as I am fully known. And now these three remain: faith, hope and love. But the greatest of these is love." 1 Cor 13*

God's love is not like our love, so anytime I write would write Rosemary a card, I always ended it with "I will love you the same" because my love was this God kind of love. Nothing could ever change that. All I ever wanted was Rosemary's love. I wanted her to be my wife and God allowed her to be my wife. And I know she belongs to God, not to me, and I am so grateful for the time that He gave me with her. I feel honored that He allowed me to see His love through her. He allowed me to see that even though her and I both made mistakes in our lives.

You may have loved ones that you are praying for. Well, I can tell you this, just love them like Christ first loved you. His love is perfect; it's beautiful. You have to do it first. You have to forgive, to love, and to be like Christ first.

> *"We love because he first loved us. Whoever claims to love God yet hates a brother or sister is a liar. For whoever does not love their brother and sister, whom they have seen, cannot love God, whom they have not seen."*
> 1 Jn 4:19-20

For those forgiven, extend forgiveness more because you remember what it was like to be forgiven.

I wish Rosemary and I could have written this book together because this is our inheritance, our legacy that we want to leave behind for our children and our children's children. It is our way of sharing the love that God had for us over and over. We wanted to share this with those around us. As God has led me to write this book, I had to include Rosemary because Rosemary was the tangible love of God to me. And even though her body is not here, her spirit is, and I will always love her the same.

PS: I Love You

Prayers For The Saints

The Call To Salvation Prayer

If anyone reading this book has not given their life to Jesus Christ and want to know that you're going to heaven, please read the prayer below and join us in the Kingdom of God.

Lord God,
I want you in my life. I need to know you. I need a relationship with you. Be my Lord. Be my savior. Forgive me for all of my sins. Thank you for sending your only begotten son, Jesus Christ, to die on the cross for me and resurrecting him. From this day forward, Jesus Christ is the Lord of my life. Forever and ever.
Amen

If you said this prayer, congratulations!, you are now a Child of God. Your life will never be the same. Please write to us and let us know you have given your life to Christ. Welcome brother and sister in Christ.

Rededication Prayer

Heavenly Father, as we come before You today, we come repenting for the times You gave us an unction to pray and we didn't. We repent for allowing things to take the place of prayer. Your Word have promised, if we confess our sins, you're faithful and just to forgive our sins, and to cleanse us from all unrighteousness. So today, we repent of our sins, we come with rededication to you. We ask in the Name of Jesus, help us to pray as You desire us to pray as Your children. Give us a hunger and thirst for righteousness, help us to enjoy being in Your presence and allowing You to work Your righteousness, Your love, Your compassion in for others, Your concerns for others in us. Help us to love You as Jesus loves You, help us to submit ourselves and our belongings to You. Help us to pray always and not faint when the prayer hasn't been answered in the time we think it should have been. Help us to have holy boldness. Help us to draw others by Your loving kindness flowing through us towards others. Today, we say yes Father, to Your Spirit, Your Word, and Your way.

In Jesus Name we ask this prayer, and we thank You Father, for hearing and answering these prayers, thank God, Amen!

Home Dedication Prayer

    The Lord said this is your home. You will be able to lay your head on your own pillow. Have peace and rest by putting Me first in your life, marriage, and family. I will be here all the time. Through good times and difficult times. Remember that all decisions will come through (*insert your name*). Listen to the Holy Spirit, He will give you the answers. You're going to hear counseling from other friends, believers, and even your dad and mom. Remember to always confirm it with the word of God. Jesus said it is written. Communication is a must! Praying together is a must! Going to church is a must! Giving God the tithe is a must! One more thing, never let your spouse turn his or her back and walk away from this home. By letting them go, you have opened the door for the enemy to move in! Keep that door closed in Jesus Christ's name. Amen!

Healing Prayer

Father, thank you that according to Your Holy Scriptures, your Son, Yeshua, took my infirmities, bore my sickness, and that by His stripes I am healed (1 Ptr 2:24). I know that you have plans for me to prosper and to be in good health. You are my Great Physician and I praise you and thank you that you desire that I be well and whole.

Thank you for taking the time to read our story and allowing us to be transparent with all of you.

We pray this book inspires you, heals you, and sets you on your God path, in Jesus Mighty Name.

God Bless,

Phillip & Rosemary Mata